CAMBRIDGE STUDIES
IN ENGLISH LEGAL HISTORY

Edited by
H. A. HOLLOND
Fellow of Trinity College, Cambridge
and sometime Rouse Ball Professor of English Law

EARLY ENGLISH
LEGAL LITERATURE

BY

T. F. T. PLUCKNETT, F.B.A.

Hon. Fellow of Emmanuel College, Cambridge
Professor of Legal History in the
University of London

CAMBRIDGE
AT THE UNIVERSITY PRESS
1958

CAMBRIDGE UNIVERSITY PRESS
Cambridge, New York, Melbourne, Madrid, Cape Town, Singapore, São Paulo, Delhi

Cambridge University Press
The Edinburgh Building, Cambridge CB2 8RU, UK

Published in the United States of America by Cambridge University Press, New York

www.cambridge.org
Information on this title: www.cambridge.org/9780521116688

First published 1958
This digitally printed version 2009

A catalogue record for this publication is available from the British Library

ISBN 978-0-521-05966-4 hardback
ISBN 978-0-521-11668-8 paperback

CONTENTS

GENERAL EDITOR'S PREFACE

THE chapters of this book were delivered in the University as Lectures commissioned by the managers of the F. W. Maitland Memorial Fund, in commemoration of the hundredth anniversary of the birth of Maitland (1850–1906). That great prestige will accrue from them to this series goes without saying. The pleasure which their publication gives to the general editor is enhanced by his awareness that it will be shared by the founder of the series, Professor H. D. Hazeltine, and its most eminent contributor, Professor Roscoe Pound, sometime Dean of the Harvard Law School. For these two scholars, both happily flourishing in retirement at Cambridge, Massachusetts, were Professor Plucknett's particular mentors, the former at Emmanuel College, Cambridge, the latter at the Harvard Law School.

H. A. H.

PREFACE

THE six chapters of this book, originally delivered as lectures in Cambridge, are here printed for the first time, save for chapter I, which appeared in the *Law Quarterly Review* for April 1951. It is now reprinted with the permission of the editor and publishers of that *Review*—where some of Maitland's earliest essays first saw the light.

It has been the theme of these lectures that there is much to learn from Maitland's writings, not merely the results which he acquired but the method and inspiration of his work. The Selden Society is 'promoting the knowledge and study of English legal history' by reprinting the contents of the *Collected Papers*, one volume of which has already appeared under the editorship of Professor Helen Cam, who has contributed a very useful bibliography. Other volumes will follow, and will contain papers of more technical legal interest. It is also bringing out a collection of *Letters* which will prove to be of considerable interest.

In promoting these lectures, and in making his writings again accessible, the Memorial Fund and the Selden Society have both contributed to the fame of a very great scholar. It is for us his readers and admirers to carry on his work.

T. F. T. P.

CHAPTER I

MAITLAND'S VIEW OF LAW
AND HISTORY

THERE was once a time when every university had its own calendar, bright with the feasts of its own particular saints. In 1536, however, colleges were warned by a canon of convocation that holy days degenerate into holidays which are the occasion of 'sloth and idleness' and 'licentious vacation'. Observances were therefore much abridged. Centenaries, fortunately, seem not to be within the act; hence if we avoid the 'excess and riot' which so grieved the paternal heart of Henry VIII, there seems no harm in our innocent celebration of this anniversary.

There is even profit to be had in it. It is good to obey the generous instinct to praise famous men; it is better still to re-examine their works; and it is by far the best to profit from their examples and carry on their work. That simple and salutary pro-gramme is no light matter when we fix our minds upon Frederic William Maitland. To praise him is indeed easy. Has any other man living or dead, English or foreign, made seisin (for example) an entertaining subject? Everything he wrote exercises a deep fascination and a personal attraction, making Sunday tramps of us all. But who shall evaluate that astonishing shelf-full of books? Indeed, is it credible that one man could write them in the space of two and twenty years? It would certainly be appropriate on this occasion to take each of them and severally assess its contribution to the accumulated store of English legal history, but it would need a committee or an academy to do it. The man who feels entitled to give an opinion on *Domesday Book and Beyond* might speak with less confidence of *English Law and the Renaissance* or of 'Trust and Corporation'. Clearly, we must call in the legal, constitu-tional, economic, ecclesiastical, civilian, and all the other experts, and let each of them survey his own province.

Having done that, we should still be very careful how we inter-pret the experts' evidence. When we are told that the garrison theory of borough origins is no longer in favour, for example, shall we get rid of our copy of *Township and Borough*? If we are

assured on high authority, with persuasive arguments, that Os-
wald's leases should be treated as evidence of the absence, rather
than of the presence, of feudalism in the days of King Edgar, shall
we therefore abandon *Domesday Book and Beyond*? The answer is
obviously, no. Several reflexions arise on this matter. The first of
them is well expressed by Maitland himself in his obituary essay
upon Stubbs—a grave and judicious tribute to the master, but
also a subtly revealing indication of Maitland's own mind. In
that essay,[1] he remarks that most of Stubbs's writing had been in
the field of general narrative or biography, until at the end he
closed his historical labours with the great *Constitutional History*.
Of that great classic Maitland praised the immense scope, and
then the enormous mass of material, and then—

the risks that are run, especially in the earlier chapters. This last is a
point that may not be quite obvious to all; but is it not true that the
historian runs greater and more numerous dangers if he tells of the
growth and decay of institutions than if he writes a straightforward
narrative of events? Would Gibbon's editor find so few mistakes to
rectify if Gibbon had seriously tried to make his readers live for a while
under the laws of Franks and Lombards?

Maitland knew very well that he was running risks; he did not
expect to come through unscathed. That is the common lot of
legal and institutional historians, and those who feel bound, after
due reflexion, to make a point against Maitland, remember that
they too are vulnerable.

There is more in it than that, however. The risks and the scratches
are part of the daily work of institutional history. Stubbs himself
warned us to be prepared for tracing subterranean streams if we
embark upon his *Select Charters*. What matters more than any
particular mishap is the spirit of the adventurer. Did he understand clearly what he was about? Did he furnish himself with the
proper equipment? Was he skilled in its use? Above all, had he
the qualities of mind and temper which are essential in such an
undertaking? When we weigh the answers to those questions, we
can hardly doubt that Maitland was superlatively well equipped
and finely constituted for the hazards of institutional history. In
every book and article of his, whether it be massive or slight, there
is instruction for us who can watch a master at work, displaying

---

[1] Maitland, *Collected Papers*, III, 495, from *English Historical Review*, 1905.

all his skill and resource, courage and candour, in a great intellectual adventure. Let no one think that he can neglect anything that Maitland wrote, for yet another reason which is this: his work is remarkably fertile in suggestions. Sometimes he would obviously open up whole realms of novel study, but on numberless occasions he has left mere hints to express his doubts upon a point which needs more study. The hints are very gently expressed, not at all obvious, but well worth looking for. Maitland took a delight in manipulating language and was careful about mood and tense. An impersonal construction, which dissociates him from the statement which follows, may very well indicate a doubt or a question which at the moment he was unable to pursue further.[1] For the discerning reader there are many clues well worth following up.

The more one reads Maitland, the more conscious one becomes of these 'inner parts' in his writing—and that raises the question of his style. This is a difficult matter. In the sense that Gibbon or Blackstone had a style, we must say that Maitland had none. He adopted no model and submitted to no tradition. It would seem, from reading any page of his, that he deliberately refrained from the slightest hint of formality, of discipline, or of classical influence. But he avoided jargon and professional cant like the plague. He could delve deep into the mysteries of jurisprudence and still write English—even with Gierke before his eyes. If a writer produced a pretentious book there was a word for him: 'mountainous jackass'. The splendid epithet is indeed Lord Acton's, but Maitland recorded it and cherished it.[2]

This does not mean that Maitland was indifferent to style. His notice of Stubbs[3] shows how sensitive he could be to phrase and structure and to the architecture of a book. His own nature imposed upon him a different sort of expression. It is relevant here to say that his schooling was unfortunate in this respect. At Eton he learned 'to hate Greek and its alphabet and its accents and its accidence and its syntax and its prosody, and all its appurtenances'.[4] An astonishing result, for Maitland had a deep love of languages, and was fascinated by their odd little ways. German was a delight to him. Anglo-Norman yielded up its uncouth

---

[1] Thus, the words 'It is regarded as...' introduce a view of Westminster II c. 24 which Maitland refrained from sanctioning with his approval; cf. 'Case and the Statute of Westminster II', *Columbia Law Review*, XXXI, 779.

[2] Maitland, *Collected Papers*, III, 514.

[3] *Ibid.* p. 505.   [4] H. A. L. Fisher, *Frederic William Maitland*, p. 5.

secrets when he unravelled the queer and complex accidence of Year-Book French. Philologists still speak with respect of his famous introduction,[1] and refer to 'Maitland's Law'. Nor was all that labour merely utilitarian, for he was deeply interested in language for its own sake; as he lay ill long after in the 'Fortunate Isles' he delighted in the justly famed subtleties of the subjunctive in Spanish.[2]

The study of the classics, which has played so large a part in the formation of style in Europe, by some mischance passed Maitland by. His love of words remained, and on almost every page one can see him choosing them with care, arranging them effectively (sometimes rather fancifully), making them do what he wants, and yet respecting their personalities so that they seem to enjoy doing it. Every page leaves the impression that it was written with delight. Maitland took words seriously, moreover; every word has a history—which is a very serious matter, for the history of words sometimes illuminates (and sometimes obscures) the history of legal thought.

The essence of Maitland's style, therefore, seems to be its foundation upon the word rather than upon the sentence or the period. He seems to have tamed them enough to be useful, but not enough to make them march with a Roman tramp, or to perform the evolutions of a verbal ballet. He handles them in small groups rather than in massed formations. It will be noticed how easy it is to read Maitland aloud; there is plenty of space to take breath, and so the sentence runs all the swifter. He wrote as if he were speaking, and he was in fact a remarkable speaker. As an undergraduate he delighted the Union with glittering speeches, and when he wrote it was neither a dissertation, nor an oration, but the nimble informal impromptu which got down on to paper. The effect is therefore one of gay intimacy with a lively companion. The attraction is irresistible; on the one hand the matter and the thought, on the other the ceaseless gambol of the words. He wrote at high speed—how else could he have done so much?—and yet it is rare for his restlessness to tire, and very rare indeed for the words to get out of hand.[3] One last remark, which may or may

---

[1] Prefixed to *Y.B. 1 & 2 Edward II* (Selden Society); partly reprinted in *Cambridge History of English Literature*, I, 407–12. Cf. Fisher, *op. cit.* 166–7.

[2] Fisher, *op. cit.* p. 136.

[3] *Collected Papers*, I, 487, lines 7–8, strike one reader as infelicitous.

not carry with it a criticism: on no account should one imitate Maitland's style.

From the style we pass to the man, and turn again to the question which was before us a moment ago. The risks of undertaking institutional history are not to be despised; we may allow for the misadventures which must befall the pioneer in unexplored territory; we are still left with the spirit and temper of the adventurer. The attempt to recapture that spirit and to appreciate its true nature and its real significance is essential to an understanding of Maitland, and of his view of law and history. Indeed, the inquiry ought to carry us further even than that, for at the root of it all lies the question of the relations of history and English law, and the relations of English law and the universities.

Much later in his career, Maitland brought these questions into focus in his inaugural lecture when in 1888 he became Downing Professor. Of that searching, anxious and even despondent discourse more must be said in a moment. It bore the challenging title 'Why the History of English Law is not written'. The first part of his career culminated in that question, and the imperfect answer which he suggested. The second part is occupied with the abandonment of some of the answers of 1888 and, of course, with the magnificent solution when, in 1895, the history of English law *was* written.

By way of preliminary, it will be well to inquire into the state of English legal history when Maitland was still a student. There was only one book of any size which treated English legal history as a subject in its own right, independently of an exposition of modern law, and that was the work of John Reeves. The first edition of the first volume came out in 1783; by 1814 the story down to 1603 was told in five volumes. That the book is abominably technical[1] is obvious at once. But it should be equally obvious that it could not be otherwise when one thinks of the state of the law in 1814. No doubt the historian's true function is to reconstruct the past as it was, and to show us the things that mattered to the people who had to live with them; yet the historian cannot altogether escape the influence of his own day, and is therefore bound to emphasize elements in the past which seem to bear upon

---

[1] In the preface to the first edition, Reeves described his book as 'an introductory work...intelligible to a person unacquainted with law books...a simple narrative'.

his own contemporary scene. The law in Reeves's day was in the last stages of dissolution. What else could Reeves do but patiently trace the history of all the sundry items piled up in the wreckage of the ages which constituted English law in 1814? Patient he was, and spent nigh half a lifetime in his incredibly dull, but immensely useful work.

Reeves's book had one other characteristic: it was very insular. In 1869 a lawyer of some note in his day, W. F. Finlason, undertook to remedy this. He brought out a new edition furnished with numerous notes which were always patronizing, and sometimes rude, to Reeves. His notes at times are valuable, but often are inspired by his particular crotchet that Roman law survived, uninterrupted by all the invasions, and that it is the source of all that is worth anything in the common law.[1] Finlason's inspiration here is Guizot, but he is always ready to correct his masters, and when Guizot cautiously excluded England from his generalization, Finlason adds his customary footnote 'this is a mistake'.[2] Wrongheaded as he was,[3] Finlason did have the merit of bringing English law into some sort of historical contact with Europe, but do what he would, he could neither romanticize nor Romanize the tough and technical Reeves. In later years Maitland and Holdsworth gave Reeves his due; but it is unthinkable that Reeves should have attracted anyone to the study of legal history. If ever the history of English law was to be written it would be with a different view of history, and a very different view of law.

There was nothing yet in print to tempt a young man into the study of English legal history. Certainly the idea had not yet crossed Maitland's mind, for at the university he read mental and moral science. His ambition was to lead an academic life as a political scientist. He competed for a fellowship in this field, but unsuccessfully. Regretfully, we may well believe, he left Cambridge and read for the bar. Law was not his first choice for a career, but he became in a short time a very accomplished practitioner in the peculiar art of conveyancing. There were competent judges in this matter who thought highly of Maitland's legal abilities, but they doubted whether he was quite the sort of man who would

[1] 'All that was worth anything in [the common law] was derived from the civil law': Reeves, *History of the English Law* (ed. Finlason), I, cxiii, n. 1.

[2] *Ibid.* I, cxix, n. 1.

[3] A particularly flagrant example is when he reproves the learned Reeves for not believing the *Mirror of Justices*: Reeves (ed. Finlason), I, 41 n.

make a success of legal practice. In that small but highly competitive world learning and ability may not be quite enough; it was felt that Maitland's many gifts and advantages did not include the vulgar art of 'getting on'. Besides, real property law had not won his respect. Coming from the cold clear light of Henry Sidgwick's classroom, much of the intricate erudition which he had so swiftly mastered looked to him rather like solemn nonsense—indeed, mischievous nonsense. The law was in a very unsatisfactory state, and he soon discovered why. The blame rested on its history, or rather, on the survival of institutions and rules which had long since ceased to be useful.

To the unhistorical mind there is often a romantic attraction in the survival of odd things from the past. Many lawyers take pleasure in recounting some queer rule which defies all reason, but is certainly old. To a historian such a thing is revolting. The fact that Maitland said so in his first published article in 1879 is clear evidence that by that early date Maitland was already at heart a historian. The article[1] in question is a dazzling invective against primogeniture and the heir-at-law. Nowhere has Maitland concentrated so much indignation, ridicule and erudition as in these glittering pages. He attacks these institutions as being 'some sort of *fantasia* or *capriccio* on the *Leges Barbarorum*'. Not only does he echo Bentham and applaud the audacities of Joshua Williams, but he proceeds still further and attacks the Historical School—which can be regarded as crowning proof of his historical maturity—and confesses with mock humility that he is possibly behind this latest fashion of 'an age whose chief ambition is to be behind itself'. Beside all the rhetoric and indignation against the shocking state of real property law, there is also considerable erudition. Maitland had been reading Brunner's famous work on the ancient *Anglonormannische Erbfolgesystem*, had followed the famous feud of the *Gradualisten* and *Parentelisten*, and had realized that beneath all the technicalities of different systems of inheritance there lies the vital institution of the family. It was apparent to him, moreover, that there is a deep fascination in the study of living things while they are alive, but that when they are dead, they ought to be decently buried. To him it was not a matter for sentimental pride, but a disgrace, that a learned German in search of primitive (and indeed pre-historic) law should find it

[1] Maitland, *Collected Papers*, I, 162 (from the *Westminster Review*).

perambulating Lincoln's Inn in the 42nd year of Victoria like a zombie—completely dead, yet capable of causing endless trouble and multitudinous costs.[1] That was an attack upon law; legal history was a very different matter. 'If we want barbarism at its best,' he wrote, 'we can turn to the *Lex Salica*; if we want scholasticism at its best, we prefer Thomas Aquinas to Lord Coke.'[2]

That was the state of Maitland's thought in 1879. The disappointed philosopher of 1875 had become the indignant conveyancer of 1879 who had lost his respect for real property law. But he had found legal history, and henceforth he turned with eager interest to 'barbarism at its best'. In 1881 he produced a penetrating study of kindred and blood-feud in the ancient laws of Wales; in 1882 came a paper on the criminal liability of the hundred; in 1883 the English Year Books and the French *Olim* were woven into a history of malice aforethought. These three essays[3] all show the characteristics of Maitland's approach—the concentration on the origins and roots of problems, and the broad comparative apparatus of English, Celtic, Germanic, Scandinavian, Norman and French material. In that same year 1883 he made up his mind to abandon legal practice if possible and so became a candidate for the Readership in Law at Oxford. Again he was disappointed, but the vocation to legal history took an ever firmer hold upon him and he pressed on; in 1884 appeared his first book, the *Pleas of the Crown of Gloucester*.

At this point another name enters the story, Paul Vinogradoff. They met first on a 'Sunday tramp' in January 1884 and then corresponded, apparently about the state of Bracton's text. On Sunday, 11 May 1884, occurred a 'decisive meeting' between them at Oxford, at which Maitland, it is said, first learned from the lips of a foreigner the matchless riches of the Public Record Office.

His vivid mind was instantly made up: on the following day he returned to London, drove to the Record Office and...asked for the earliest plea roll of the county of Gloucester. He was supplied with a roll for the year 1221 and without any formal training in palaeography proceeded to puzzle it out and to transcribe it.[4]

Maitland himself is vouched for this story, but it is none the less impossible to accept it. His progress at the bar was impeded

---

[1] *Collected Papers*, I, 174.   [2] *Ibid.* I, 190.
[3] *Ibid.* I, 202, 230, 304.   [4] Fisher, *Maitland*, pp. 24–5.

by his inability to assert himself, and he seems as if constitution-
ally impelled to give others exaggerated credit for their small share
in his own work. His memory of Vinogradoff's early influence
must surely have erred. The whole story can be refuted from
evidence printed by Mr Fisher who himself gave it currency. There
is a letter dated 28 April 1884 (*before* the momentous meeting),
in which Maitland anticipates with pleasure a paper by Vinogradoff on the text of Bracton, and continues:

> I have written for Pollock a paper about seisin and had occasion to
> deal with a bit of Bracton which, as printed, is utter rubbish. I therefore
> looked at some of the MSS. and found that the blunder was an old one.
> I shall not have occasion to say any more than that there are manu-
> scripts which make good sense of the passage.[1]

It is immediately obvious that Maitland had been puzzling out
manuscripts before the crucial meeting. It might seem, however,
that Maitland has got his tenses mixed: 'I have written a paper...'
but 'I shall not have occasion to say any more...': in fact his
strict accuracy in these tenses can be established. The paper had
been finished, and sent off to Pollock, presumably as editor of the
Law Quarterly Review; when it was printed,[2] the note about the
manuscripts was added as a postscript, and not inserted into the
body of the article. We are thus bound to take Maitland's words
in their strict sense and tense: he had written the paper on seisin
before the crucial meeting.[3] Now when we look at that paper what
do we find? We find this, that Maitland has already been to Chancery
Lane, searched the plea rolls of early Henry III, and given
references to them by number, year, term and membrane. The
proof is complete. With that established, the legend that the *Pleas
of the Crown of Gloucester* was the direct result of the meeting of
11 May can be shortly dismissed as impossible. To begin with, it
involves not one roll but two, which Maitland collated, showing
that the tidy roll has a worse text than the badly written roll. The
collated rolls with a few notes run to 155 large pages; then there
is a very solid introduction of 50 pages more (which refers to other

---

[1] *Ibid.* pp. 37–8.
[2] *Law Quarterly Review*, I, 324 (reprinted in *Collected Papers*, I, 329).
[3] Evidently he had also parted with it, and quite possibly it was already in
type, so that the new matter could only appear as a postscript. The prudent
editor of the first volume would naturally have made sure of the material of his
first three or more issues before launching the *Review* in the first place.

eyre rolls incidentally). Could any man have done all that, found a publisher, had the book set up, marked the proofs, had it printed and bound, so that it was published in the second half of November[1] six months later? It is manifestly incredible. We have just seen proof from his own letter that he had been working on plea rolls before the momentous date: it is inescapable that he was also engaged upon the Gloucester pleas at the same time.

The summer of 1884 therefore contains no sudden conversion to legal history in general, or to plea rolls in particular; but it is marked by Maitland's abandonment of practice to come back to Cambridge as Reader in English Law. He had not forgotten his early studies in Cambridge. After nearly a year's law-teaching, he wrote to Alfred Marshall, the economist, in a letter (*penes me*) dated 13 March 1885:

> Sometimes I wish that I could give up lecturing about law and once more prepare myself for the Moral Science Tripos at your feet and Sidgwick's.[2]

No doubt there were regrets, but Maitland remained loyal to his second choice, and from that year onwards comes the astonishing series of books, each of them a capital contribution to some fundamental and difficult subject, and each of them inaugurating new and fruitful lines of research for his successors. The four years of his readership were mainly occupied by the enormous task of editing *Bracton's Note Book* which Vinogradoff had not only discovered, but quickly identified. Maitland transcribed all but thirty of the one thousand four hundred printed pages, and furnished it with an introductory volume which includes a superb set of indexes and tables which could only have been produced by a complete master of medieval law.

Even more important was the foundation in 1887 of the Selden Society whose sole object is 'to encourage the study and advance the knowledge of the history of English Law'. There was widespread support among the highest in the land; no one doubted that the object was worthy of the most distinguished and sincere

---

[1] It appeared 'between 15 and 29 November'; *Publishers' Circular* (1884), p. 1297.

[2] Years later, it was Henry Sidgwick who encouraged Maitland to embark upon Gierke; Otto Gierke, *Political Theories of the Middle Age* (tr. Maitland), p. xlv, n. 5.

patronage. But goodwill alone is not sufficient to produce a volume a year, especially when the subscriptions do not quite meet the bills. A still more serious difficulty, however, is apparent from the list of publications. The first volume (1887) is edited by Maitland. The second volume (1888) is edited by Maitland also. The third was by Baildon, but the fourth (in spite of the title page) is all Maitland. Maitland supplied single-handed three-quarters of the Society's output. There were not enough qualified men to do the work in those early years.

In the year 1888 Maitland was elected to the Downing chair of English law, and was called upon for the customary inaugural lecture. That lecture[1] is the only thing he ever wrote which publicly reveals the keenness of his disappointment at the prospects of legal history. He took as the title 'Why the history of English law is not written'. The inquiry led him to some very important fundamental considerations, but it is easy to excuse some of his pessimism by remembering that he was now carrying the Selden Society on his shoulders, and that, besides the general problem of academic apathy in England, there was the particular problem 'Why the Selden Society cannot find editors'.

Deep at the roots of the question, Maitland found certain irreconcilable contradictions which make it especially hard for a man trained exclusively in English law to become a historian. In the first place, English law was isolated from every other study and was traditionally taught at the Inns, although everything else was taught at the universities.

The law which this school evolved stood us in good stead; it was the bridge which carried us safely from the medieval to modern times, and we will speak well of it. But one thing it could not do, it could not possibly produce its own historian. History involves comparison, and the English lawyer who knew nothing and cared nothing for any system but his own hardly came in sight of the idea of legal history.

That is a hard saying, but it was true then, and it is true now. Then there is the pseudo-historicity of our law. Occasionally (but very occasionally) it is necessary for practical reasons to go far back in time to find authority:

A lawyer finds on his table a case about rights of common which sends him to the Statute of Merton. But is it really the law of 1236

---

[1] Published separately, but reprinted in *Collected Papers*, I, 480.

that he wants to know? No, it is the ultimate result of the interpretations set on the statute by the judges of twenty generations. That process... is from the lawyer's point of view an evolution of the true intent and meaning of the old law: from the historian's point of view it is almost of necessity a process of perversion and misunderstanding. Thus we are tempted to mix up two different logics, the logic of authority, and the logic of evidence. What the lawyer wants is authority and the newer the better; what the historian wants is evidence and the older the better.... A mixture of legal dogma and legal history is in general an unsatisfactory compound.... The lawyer must be orthodox, otherwise he is no lawyer; an orthodox history seems to me a contradiction of terms. If this truth is hidden from us by current phrases about 'Historical methods of legal study' that is another reason why the history of our law is unwritten. If we try to make history the handmaid of dogma she will soon cease to be history.

In that passage Maitland claimed to be only stating an obvious truism, and he seems to have thought that those few words of warning were sufficient. His own mind changed gear smoothly and silently, and he assumed that lawyers generally, when their attention had been drawn to the matter, would find no difficulty in doing likewise.[1]

He directed most of his attention to the immediately practical obstacles in writing English legal history, and here we seem to get echoes of anxious council meetings of the Selden Society. In the first place he observes that a man may be an excellent lawyer and still be innocent of legal history. That is an obvious fact, and very fortunately so. Maitland then proceeds to the converse and notes that 'a thorough training in modern law is almost indispensable for any one who wishes to do good work on legal history'. He feels this so strongly that he proceeds to state it more explicitly: 'I do not think that an Englishman will often have the patience to study medieval procedure and conveyancing unless he has had to study modern procedure and conveyancing, and to study them professionally.' And there indeed was the heart of the problem; a competent lawyer has high hopes of being too busy in practice to have leisure for legal history. From professional lawyers Maitland drew no hope. Experience has confirmed that conclusion.

'What, then, can the universities do?' The hopes of his audience were quickly dashed. First, the business of a law school is to

---

[1] For a historian's comment (from a rather different standpoint) on the relations of law and history, see W. Stubbs, *Lectures on Early English History*, p. 37.

teach law, and 'we should not wish to see a professor of law breaking and entering the close of the professor of history'. Secondly, the aspiring legal historian should take the law tripos, read in chambers and acquire some practice. Thirdly, he will not get much law anyhow in his two years' tripos work. Fourthly, the law faculty is understaffed. Fifthly, his final comment was that the only incentive which had so far produced results had been not the tripos, but the Yorke Prize; we needed more prizes, and perhaps a higher degree in law, since 'potentates and politicians' had made off with the LL.D.

'Where then lies our trust? Perhaps in failure.' When the young barrister finally realizes that he has no future at the bar, 'in that day of tribulation may it be remembered that the history of English law has not been written'. Even then, perhaps, our imaginary student is not he that should come; well, there is plenty of hard gruelling work to be done, and at the end he may earn a footnote of gratitude from the great man when he does appear. Finally, with an acid anecdote of what a Lord Chief Justice said about a professor of law, Maitland concluded what he justly called his long and dismal discourse.

Has ever an academic audience heard so disconcerting an inaugural? Maitland was already ill; in his article[1] on 'The Shallows and Silences of Real Life' he saw with remarkable prescience some of the less happy results of the Local Government Act of 1888; and of course there was always the perilous position of the Selden Society. He was clearly in a mood of deep depression.

Our concern at this moment, however, is the fundamental wrongness of his assumptions and analysis. The inaugural marks a stage in his mental history because it still shows an imperfect view of the place of legal history. As we shall see, his later career must be read as the gradual abandonment of the propositions laid down in 1888.

Thus, the proposal that legal history must be annexed to the study of law is entirely misconceived. Maitland had himself just shown that their material, their method, and their logic were incompatible, and that there was no necessity for a lawyer, *qua* lawyer, bothering with history. To make legal history the preserve of professional lawyers is indeed to condemn it to extinction. As for his requirement of legal training and experience of practice,

---

[1] *Collected Papers,* I, 476.

what of Stubbs, whose handling of law Maitland admired so much that he almost wished he had been a judge?[1] What too of Vinogradoff, who had never been a lawyer of any sort? We must also ask why he should forbid the lawyer to break and enter the close of the historian. Once again we have to invoke his fundamental distinction between legal and historical method. Once the professor of law embarks upon legal history he has become a historian, for legal history is not law, but history. And so the legal historian commits no trespass in the pleasant fields of history— he is treading his own soil. Later in his career Maitland himself was to enter boldly and joyously into the very heart of general history—to his evident delight, and for our lasting instruction and enjoyment.

Shorn of these misconceptions, the inaugural still poses the fundamental problem: the completely opposite aims and methods of the lawyer and the legal historian are inherent in the very natures of history and of English law. There was the fatal danger that legal history might be asked to produce, not the truth, but some pious legend which should be useful in settling some point of current law. 'If we try to make history the handmaid of dogma, she will soon cease to be history.'

That peril is much greater now than it was when Maitland spoke. In our own day it is distressingly frequent for law students to begin their legal studies very young, with the result that their first and only experience of systematic thought is obtained within the peculiar framework of English law. Prolonged subjection to that influence makes it exceptionally hard for the well-trained lawyer to think like a historian. If Maitland underestimated this difficulty, it must have been because he had never experienced it, although obviously he had observed it in others. His own mind had not been formed in legal studies, and the law was not his first choice. He was in fact one of those 'failures' to whom he looked for the salvation of legal history. He brought to the law a mind exercised in the wide open spaces of philosophy—and how deeply he revolted against the confinement of his chambers is written large in the boisterous and angry paper on real property published in 1879.

As we approach the last phase of his career the pace quickens to an incredible speed. The feeble Selden Society got afloat when a

---

[1] *Collected Papers*, III, 503.

small band of recruits had been enlisted and trained, notably G. J. Turner, mathematician and briefless barrister, who became a legal historian of considerable achievement and a devoted friend of Maitland's last days. Volume after volume appeared under his direction ranging over an enormous field of law and history. He himself edited plea rolls for the Pipe Roll Society (1891), a parliament roll for the Rolls Series (1893), and *Bracton and Azo* for the Selden Society (1894). But all these were merely chips from the workshop where the *magnum opus* was being fashioned. It appeared the next year (1895) in two huge volumes: at long last the history of English law was written. Tremendous fragments left over became *Domesday Book and Beyond* (1896) and *Township and Borough* (1898). Meantime he collected a set of articles on *Canon Law* (1898), and was publishing as articles works which ought to be reprinted as books—three articles on seisin (1885–8),[1] three more on the Register of Writs,[2] and most recently five papers on trust and corporation,[3] with the translation of Gierke (1900) to match.

It would seem as though Maitland in these last years was gathering together the various threads of his experience in order to weave a richer and more colourful fabric than ever before. The papers on Gierke and corporate personality recall his early interest in political philosophy, but there was more to come. In 1900 he published the 'Elizabethan Gleanings'.[4] It is a difficult question whether a gleaner is a trespasser, but it is impossible to escape the conclusion that this time the professor of law was busy making profit in the close of the professor of history—and thoroughly enjoying himself. One of the unhappy principles in the inaugural of 1888 was thus overruled.

By the turn of the century the Selden Society had become a flourishing institution which could afford the occasional luxury of an 'extra volume'. Maitland now laid upon it the immense task of preparing critical editions of the Year Books of Edward II. Characteristically he himself devised the method, edited the first three volumes and nearly finished the fourth. His introduction to the first gave him scope for another of his trespasses—this time into the field of philology, and the history of language. Reference has already been made to the revealing obituary

---

[1] *Ibid.* I, 329, 358, 407.   [2] *Ibid.* II, 110.
[3] *Ibid.* III, 210, 244, 271, 304, 321.   [4] *Ibid.* III, 157.

notice of Stubbs which Maitland wrote in 1901. Therein he observed that Stubbs had shown from the first a remarkable power of delineating character and of managing the long unwinding narrative of political and diplomatic history, but that he deferred until the years of his maturity the 'risks that must be run' in institutional history. The result was that Stubbs's last work, the *Constitutional History of England*, was 'marvellously concrete'. It must have been in Maitland's mind when he wrote those words that his own career had run in the opposite direction. In the first flush of his vocation to legal history he had volunteered for the dangerous duty of institutional history. From the barbaric he had proceeded to the abstractions of seisin, and the procedural technicalities of the register of writs. After that, the metaphysics of corporate personality seemed almost light relief. Such matters are indeed the foundations of legal history, but prolonged contemplation of them may warp the judgment. Maitland knew this. By the time he was writing the *History of English Law* he was profoundly conscious of it, and constantly reminds his readers that dogmas and abstractions are the work of ordinary mortal men, and that if history is to be 'concrete' it must explain those abstractions in terms of human life and work. From the *persona ficta* Maitland thus proceeded to the natural man, and so 'logic yields to life, protesting all the time that it is only becoming more logical'.[1] It was the Year Books that wrought this final stage and made Maitland's work, like Stubbs's, 'marvellously concrete'. It was in their pages that Maitland came to realize the extent to which our law was a manifestation of our medieval lawyers, their Inns, and their law schools, and to stress the fact that these lay scholars had great significance in English social and intellectual life.[2]

By then, Maitland had so enlarged the bounds of legal history that the separatism of his inaugural had completely vanished. He had finally established the fact that legal history is not law, but history, and that all history is one. At the end, he wrote general history for the second volume of the *Cambridge Modern History* and was indeed invited to succeed Acton in the Regius chair of Modern History.

That, however, brings us near the end of Maitland's long pilgrimage, long yet so swiftly accomplished, a mere twenty-two

[1] *Y.B. 1 & 2 Edward II* (Selden Society), p. xix.
[2] *Ibid.* p. xxxi.

years as reader and professor here. But what a revolution he wrought! When he first turned his thoughts to the history of English law he found it the trivial annals of an insular system, designed to furnish facile explanations of the inexplicable, a picturesque excuse for intellectual lethargy, a meagre collection of professional gossip. Revolted by this sham-Gothic, Maitland turned to 'barbarism at its best'. Detesting its insularity he joined forces with Brunner, Stubbs, Holmes, Thayer, Ames, Vinogradoff, Viollet, Liebermann, Gierke, and how many others, in maintaining that English legal history can only be studied in comparison with that of other systems: 'history involves comparison'. And having brought our legal history into the main stream of European history, he finally threw down the barriers he himself had erected and liberated it from the old fetters which bound it to the faculty of law.

Technically, that is where we stand today—at least where we ought to stand. But do we? Are we quite sure that there is no need for another lecture on 'Why the history of English law is not read'? If one may judge by opinions recently expressed by men of high eminence, Maitland's view of law and history is by no means generally held. It is still too often said that English law can only be understood historically. Now English law may be bad, but is it really as bad as that? Is the law of contract unintelligible without the history of *indebitatus assumpsit*? Is tort a closed book to those who do not understand the history of trespass on the case? Surely not. But then another will get up and say, 'if that is so, why bother about legal history?'.

Why, indeed? It had been Maitland's mission to separate law from legal history, and to make certain that history should not be 'the handmaid of dogma'. He did this because the whole method and mode of thought differed in the two subjects. The real question is not whether we should teach legal history, but whether we can give to students law, and nothing but law, and still call it a liberal education. Here we wish there were more in Maitland's published papers about his idea of a university. The little that has got into print[1] shows that he did not regard it as the university's function to duplicate or usurp the work of the professional bodies in qualifying men for practice. Nobody is bound to come to a university to study English law, and indeed he must go elsewhere to get his qualification to practice. Does not that indicate an answer?

[1] *Collected Papers*, III, 419.

The university can offer something different from a professional qualification, something that will not make him a better lawyer, but a better man. In this connexion Maitland coupled jurisprudence with legal history; of the one he said 'it would give our ...men a liberal and liberating influence in their study of English law'. Of the other he said that a student can 'be made a happy man for life by an interest in what can be the most enthralling of all studies'. Can one ask more of one's studies than 'liberation' and 'happiness'? Ought a university to give anything less?

It is curious that jurisprudence should have become compulsory, for many students are not naturally fitted for it. Jurisprudence, in effect, is the product of a philosopher surveying the law, and a law student who has a philosophical cast of mind will revel in the subject. To the rest, it will be unreal and meaningless. For most students it is much easier to acquire a historical interest, and legal history is a good alternative for those who feel no call to philosophy. It shares with jurisprudence the great merit of bringing a completely different method and approach to students who are heavily pressed by the peculiar technique of English law. Both subjects get completely outside the law, and survey it and criticize it from a distance. The historian's view, and the philosopher's view, are both equally valid, but here we are concerned with the former. It ranges from 'barbarism at its best' to the latest civil code,[1] it embraces the alien thought of other ages as well as of other peoples, it is 'marvellously concrete', it has a wholesome discipline of critical thought, it is one with all other history, exact and yet humane. Above all, the barriers are down and the common is unenclosed. Here the lawyer will meet the historians of all other sorts of human activity and recognize them as fellow-commoners. This is indeed 'liberal and liberating' and enough to make any man 'happy for life'. We owe it to Maitland.

[1] *Collected Papers*, III, 474.

ADDENDUM. It is instructive to compare Maitland's Inaugural *Why the History of English Law is not Written* (1888) with the similar lament of Jacques Flach in his Introduction to *Les Origines de la France* (4 volumes, Paris, 1886–1917), where he says: 'Il faut donc en convenir: nous n'avons pas d'histoire du droit français.' Flach analyses the situation and blames 'la visée professionelle qui domine'.

CHAPTER II

THE EARLY LITERATURE OF
· ENGLISH LAW

THE modern legal text-book is a comparatively recent form. In the Middle Ages Bracton came near, and Littleton nearer still, to the modern type; but at their best they were still a long way off from the spirit and method of the text-book as we know it today. The modern legal text-book in English is just about a hundred and fifty years old, and it is high time that someone wrote its history. When that history is written, the name of Joseph Story will be conspicuous in it.

The characteristic of the modern English text-book which concerns us at this moment is its method. It begins with a definition of its subject-matter, and proceeds by logical and systematic stages to cover the whole field. The result is to present the law in a strictly deductive framework, with the implication that in the beginning there were principles, and that in the end those principles were found to cover a large multitude of cases deducible from them. Needless to say, such a presentation of English law was fundamentally false during most of its history. Historically, our law did not always proceed from principles to details, from the general to the particular. On the contrary, during most of its past, our law was a farrago of detailed instances which defied any scheme of arrangement, save perhaps the alphabetical. Nor need we assume that a modern text-book, however logically presented, was invariably composed in that way in the first place. The system of authority which now governs our law places upon an author the complicated task of discovering the substance of his book by a method which is essentially inductive, but having done so, of presenting it to the reader in a form which is deductive.

There need be no regrets about that. On the contrary, the result has been beneficent, for the combination of the two approaches to law has done much to reconcile the natural divergence between theory and practice—between life and logic, as Maitland expressed it.[1] Furthermore there has been a new and recent 'Reception';

---

[1] Above, p. 16, at n. 1; cf. Holmes, *Common Law*, 1.

the courts have made their peace with the text-writers, now that a generation of judges and practitioners has been brought up on the great text-books and continues to use them and even to cite them. In this way the whole aspect of the law has been changed. It is now possible to say truthfully that our law consists of principles, and to treat those principles as existing in the law itself, and not merely in the speculative minds of text-writers. That is indeed a revolution, and the text-writers may well be proud of their work.

It has thus been the mission of the text-book to formulate the law in terms of principles, and by its sheer intellectual weight to impose those principles upon teachers, students, lawyers and the courts—and consequently upon the law itself. The state of our text-books is therefore an accurate index of the intellectual state of the law, and a measure of its progress towards what we regard as rationality. It is from that point of view (which on the Continent is often called 'the history of legal science') that we shall examine the development of English legal literature.

At the very outset it becomes apparent that such a subject demands considerable breadth of treatment. We have not merely England, but Europe on our hands. An island we undoubtedly were, but intellectually England and Europe had constant and intimate relations. Nor must we treat law in isolation. The mental atmosphere which could nourish books of systematic scholarship was no more confined to any one science than to any one country. It was but natural, indeed, that the finest efforts of learning, and the earliest, should be devoted to the Queen of the Sciences— Theology. Of all the fields of learning, theology certainly presented the biggest problem. Its materials were immensely bulky—the Bible, the Fathers, the Councils, to say nothing of a considerable monographic literature on particular matters coming from all the centuries. At various times, but especially with the gradual revival of learning after the dark ages, attempts were made to render this mass of material accessible, and to reduce at least some of it to manageable proportions. The governing consideration was the fact that these materials were 'authorities', and so collections took the form of anthologies of the most striking, or most useful passages. Many such collections were compiled, some large, some more modest.[1] Some were designed for elementary instruction: others concentrated upon one or another of the great debates

---

[1] Herman Kantorowicz and W. W. Buckland, *Studies in the Glossators*, p. 17.

of the age—notably the investiture contest, which set scholars exploring the nature of authority in church and state and the bases of political science. Although the field of theology was still undivided, some of these collections paid particular attention to the church's hierarchical structure and disciplinary functions, and thus foreshadow the development of canon law.

A broadly based anthology of 'authorities' was no doubt a step in the right direction: the reader was put into contact with the sources. That first step did not, however, proceed very far, and gradually the need was felt for something more than haphazard compilation, for something more like a book—in short, for some systematic classification of the material. One simple and obvious way of achieving this was for a rudimentary gloss to provide cross-references to relevant material in other parts of the collection;[1] but the better solution was to arrange the material itself, bringing together authorities bearing upon the same question.

This vital development the theologians learned from the canonists, who were the first to become acutely aware of the problem of arrangement. The traditional plan of early canonical collections was either chronological, or else an arrangement according to the nature of the sources—biblical, patristic, papal, conciliar—from which the material was derived. An early essay in the new systematic style reached the Continent from Ireland even in the eighth century,[2] but there was a long period of hesitation before canonical collections were normally cast in systematic form. Once this form was established by the canonists and adopted by the theologians, studies became deeper and more technical. Large numbers of collections began to appear. In the series of canonists great names are Regino of Prüm, whose work *De Synodalibus Causis* (906) describes an institution of the Lower Rhineland which must be put beside our own twelve senior thegns who appear *c.* 997; Burchard of Worms[3] (1012–22); Ivo of Chartres (*c.* 1094), theologian and romanist as well as canonist, author of a

---

[1] The marginal references still printed in the English Bible are an example of this method.

[2] J. de Ghellinck, *Le Mouvement théologique du XIIe siècle* (2nd ed., 1948), p. 57.

[3] In Pollock and Maitland, *History of English Law*, I, 100, where the sources of the *Leges Henrici Primi* are listed, the name of Burchard may be a slip for Ivo of Chartres (*see* Thorne, 'The assize Utrum', *Columbia Law Review*, XXXIII, 429 n. 7; Stubbs, *Lectures on Early English History*, pp. 148–9 adds a third possibility).

Decretum as well as of a *Panormia*, who made the peace between our Henry I and St Anselm; and finally, the culmination of the work of over fifty predecessors was produced by Gratian in the *Decretum* which he seems to have called the *Concordia Discordantium Canonum* when it first appeared in 1140. The superiority of Gratian over his nearest rival, Ivo of Chartres, is not merely in the bulk and richness of his *Decretum* (as it soon came to be called) but also in its approach and method. 'It marks the beginning of a new epoch in the history of canon law, which now becomes an autonomous science. In it the science of law becomes organized through the criticism of the sources and of the principles of law, through the discussion of jurisdictional and procedural rules, and by the systematic handling of the materials accumulated.'[1]

More purely theological studies followed a parallel course. Many were the collections of *flores* and *sententiae* which prepared the way for the great *Sentences* of Peter Lombard which appeared in 1150–1.[2]

By the middle of the twelfth century therefore much progress had been made by the theologians, and especially by the canonists, in the difficult art of planning a book whose subject-matter was to be the whole of a science, the material of which was enormously bulky. But they were still a long way from the modern text-book,[3] with its statement of dogmatic principle shortly supported by authorities in the footnotes. Both Gratian and Peter Lombard had reached a method which was almost the inverse of the modern. In both cases the core of their book was a collection of 'authorities'. The comments of the authors are, in theory at least, in a strictly subordinate position. The ideal was that the authorities should speak for themselves, and it was only when they were obscure, difficult or apparently discordant that the author ventured to offer his own remarks. In fact, that happened often enough, and as time went on the intervention of the compiler was felt to be increasingly necessary.

Both canonists and theologians felt the urgency of the problem presented by a conflict of authorities and resorted to various devices, including what might seem at first sight to have been an

---

[1] J. de Ghellinck, *op. cit.* pp. 204–5.

[2] The modern edition is *Petri Lombardi Libri Quatuor Sententiarum*, 4 vols. (Quaracchi, 1916).

[3] Among the civilians 'Bulgarus was among the first (or perhaps the very first) to write a juristic treatise': H. Kantorowicz and W. W. Buckland, *Studies in the Glossators*, p. 70.

imitation of Valentinian III's famous Law of Citations.[1] One of
the best attempts is that by Bernold of Constance (based, it used
to be thought, upon a lost work of the famous Hincmar of Reims)
in which sound canons of historical criticism are laid down—in
some respects curiously like the rules set out by Coke in *Heydon's
Case*.[2] A book which consisted largely of 'authorities' was indeed
bound, sooner or later, to compel its reader to interpret, and then
to harmonize, them. Bernold insists that a sound interpretation
must proceed from a knowledge of the whole text and not merely
of an extract; that one canon (or statute) must be considered
together with others, because one statute will throw light upon
another; that time, place and persons may all have to be considered;
and that the causes which produced the statute might be examined.[3]

Historical interpretation, however, was soon overshadowed by
the dialectical method. This was learnt in various ways. The
growing study of Roman law brought with it familiarity with the
distinctions and classifications which Roman lawyers had eagerly
discussed under Greek influence.[4] The early faculties of arts in the
medieval universities had no need to go to the Roman lawyers,
but got their dialectic direct from the Greeks, and it was soon clear
that the syllabus of rhetoric and logic was much too narrow to
confine so explosive a matter. Fierce conflict broke out between
the faculties of theology and arts, and for a time there was angry
and scornful language among the divinity men for the arts teachers
with their 'distinctions' and their 'syllogisms'. Matters were not
made easier by the personal rivalries aroused by the spectacular
success of Peter Abelard, one of the most effective apostles of the
new method, 'who had presumed to deduce from a few simple

---

[1] Cod. Theod. I, 4, 3. On the canonist devices, see S. Kuttner and E. Rathbone, 'Anglo-Norman canonists of the twelfth century', *Traditio*, VII, 283;
Paul Fournier and Gabriel le Bras, *Collections canoniques*, II, 337 ff.; J. de
Ghellinck, *Mouvement théologique* (2nd ed., 1948), pp. 484 ff. On the special
difficulties of using translations of Greek councils, see Fournier and Le Bras,
op. cit. I, 359.

[2] (1584) 3 Rep. 7; the medieval origins of the rules, especially as to 'equity',
are discussed in S. E. Thorne, 'The equity of a statute and Heydon's Case',
Illinois Law Review, XXXI, 202.

[3] Bernold's remarks can be seen in his *De Excommunicatis vitandis* printed in
the *Monumenta Germaniae Historica: libelli de lite*, II, 139–40 and are summarized
in de Ghellinck, *op. cit.* p. 486. For Hincmar, *De Praedestinatione* see Migne,
Patrologiae Latinae Cursus, CXXV, 413.

[4] For the adoption of Greek dialectic by the Roman lawyers, see F. Schulz,
History of Roman Legal Science, pp. 62 ff.

reflexions on grammar the first nominalist philosophy'.[1] Now the wider implications of all this may well have been largely hidden from the patient compilers of *Decreta* and *Sententiae*, but the fact remains that the task which they had undertaken compelled them to adopt eventually the dialectical method, and the method in turn forced upon their notice problems of fundamental importance.

That may seem a lengthy preamble, but if we are to appreciate English legal history justly, then we must ascertain the aims and methods of scholarly composition at the time when law-books began to appear in this country, and assess the merits of our native product in the light of contemporary technique and by comparison with the best that Europe had achieved.

At first sight the English situation looks extremely simple. We did not have the overwhelming mass of material which made the theologian's task so enormous, if only by its sheer bulk; nor did we have the bewildering variety of authorities which the canonist had to reckon with, framing his political science (and fitting the different sorts of authority into it) as he went along. Indeed, our problem was in some sense the reverse of that which oppressed Continental scholars; the real difficulty of English law-writers was to find authority of any sort. The age regarded a scholarly book as being primarily a collection, as large as possible, of authoritative texts, which were to be arranged, thereby forming the substance of the book; the compiler's role was to link the texts together, discreetly and unobtrusively; where he could not avoid it, however, he ought to tackle such problems (especially antinomies) as his material presented. Clearly a book on English law ought to be a collection of authorities. But where were the authorities?

In the reign of Henry I, however, a different spirit was abroad, and English writers made efforts, sometimes great efforts, to produce a real law-book. The most extended of these works is that which acquired in the sixteenth century the name of *Quadripartitus*. The anonymous author moved in the service of Archbishop Gerhard of York (a circle which included the famous 'Anonymous of York')[2]

---

[1] G. de Lagarde, *La Naissance de l'Esprit Laïque*, v, 39.

[2] There is now a new study by G. H. Williams, *The Anonymous of York* (Harvard Theological Studies), where a close connexion with Rouen is emphasized. It is not clear what repercussions this may have on the questions of *Quadripartitus* and the *Leges Henrici Primi*. The texts of the *Anonymous* (which G. H. Williams supplements) are edited by H. Böhmer in *Monumenta Germaniae Historica: libelli de lite*, III, 642.

and was a decidedly royalist cleric. The book he undertook to write would have taxed the skill of the most learned men of his age and country; unhappily our author was ill-equipped for such a task. He wrote Latin which Liebermann (a kindly man and a tolerant critic) described as 'dunkel', 'schwülstig', 'buntschekig', 'holprig', in short, barely comprehensible, in spite of a display of erudition from the works of Horace, Virgil, Ovid, Juvenal and Macrobius.[1]

His work can be dated 1114. Of the four parts at least which at one time the author contemplated, we may speak confidently of the first, which Liebermann has printed alongside his Anglo-Saxon laws and which is in effect a translation of them into Latin. The author's hint of some sort of arrangement, however, was not fulfilled, for he merely translates the old texts as they stand. But he does not take them in chronological order. Cnut comes first, then we are sent back to Alfred, Ine, Athelstan, Edward, Edmund, Ethelred, Edgar and Edmund in that order. Most of the private tracts are here, including the *Rectitudines Singularum Personarum*. He therefore has almost everything that is in Liebermann's vast volume, save only the earliest Kentish laws. Of his thoroughness and industry we must speak highly, but his arrangement is curious. He begins with Cnut apparently because he regards it as the most important statement of Anglo-Saxon law. Then he harks far back to King Alfred and works forward in an order which is nearly (but not quite) chronological until he gets to Edmund; then he leaps forward to William the Conqueror whose 'Emendations' he had praised in the 'Argument' to *Quadripartitus*. One can frame a number of speculations to account for this order, but they can be nothing more than speculations.

To the whole work he prefixed a *Dedicatio* which is largely devoted to an enumeration of the vicious and dissolute practices which he ascribes to his contemporaries,[2] while the *Argumentum* which follows it sings the praises of 'our august lord and Caesar Henry son of the great King William'.[3] Having bestowed derogatory remarks upon many nations,[4] the author finally discloses his plan: 'The first book contains the English laws translated into Latin; the second has certain necessary writings of our own day;

---

[1] Liebermann, *Gesetze der Angelsachsen*, III, 310.
[2] *Quadripartitus*, Ded. [16], Liebermann, *op. cit.* I, 530, makes grave accusations.
[3] *Quadr.* Arg. [16] (Liebermann, *op. cit.* I, 533).   [4] *Ibid.* [17].

the third is on the nature and conduct of causes; the fourth is about theft and the parts thereof.'¹ This is a large programme, and the author took it very seriously. As his knowledge of the subject improved, he revised his work and at least three recensions are extant. His obscure reference to 'five books' is a puzzle,² but clearly he had some glimmer of what a book should be like, for he sets before his eyes 'the old practice of the fathers as improved upon by the new cleverness of the moderns'.³

Book I is therefore in print before us in Liebermann's massive first volume. Book II is of a different sort, but is nevertheless in print, partly in Liebermann's *Gesetze*, partly in his other publications, and partly in various other places.⁴ Our author had not yet freed himself from the habit of writing pretentious and barely comprehensible prefaces; we therefore find Book II introduced by a '*Prefatio* to the decretals and new laws (*emendationes*) of Henry I'. Here in his murkiest Latin the author sets forth his ideas upon kingship.⁵ This done, he finally gets down to his text: 'Incipiunt leges Henrici regis Anglorum.'⁶ His book is in effect a collection of letters, state papers and documents of various sorts, loosely joined together with connecting portions of narrative. At the head of his documents comes the coronation charter of Henry I, followed by state papers relating to investiture, the disputes of Archbishop Gerhard of York, the celibacy of archdeacons and (rather irrelevantly) Henry I's ordinance on the county and the hundred. It may well be that the author would have liked to compile a sort of *Decretum* of English ecclesiastical law, heavily weighted in favour of the king in the investiture controversy, and in favour of York in the conflict with Canterbury.⁷

Books III and IV are a mystery. Nothing has come down to us under that description, and it would at first sight be easy to

---

¹ *Quadr.* Arg. [32] (Liebermann, *op. cit.* I, 535).
² *Ibid.* [31].   ³ *Ibid.* [31].
⁴ References in Liebermann, *op. cit.* I, 544–6.
⁵ For a free translation see Stubbs, *Early English History*, pp. 145–7.
⁶ This is not the same as the more famous *Leges Henrici Primi* discussed below, p. 27.
⁷ It is worth noting that while royalist theory was being developed at York, papal views were being elaborated at Durham: see H. S. Offler, 'The Tractate *De Iniusta Vexacione Willelmi*', *English Historical Review*, LXVI, 321. The long Canterbury–York conflict is a prominent theme in R. Foreville, *L'Eglise et la royauté* (Paris, 1943).

believe that they were never written. Yet we know that the author had a high admiration for the legal work of Henry I and his most blessed father the Conqueror, and that his ultimate aim was to produce a book of current law and not merely an antiquarian collection. We have evidence, too, of his dogged determination to master his subject and accomplish his task—he had three attempts at *Quadripartitus* and visibly improved each time:[1] but he was severely handicapped by imperfect English and abominable Latin, and a too great ambition drove him to write in the clerkly tongue instead of in French which was seemingly the only language which came at all naturally to him.

Instead of the third book which he had projected on 'causes' and a fourth on theft, the indefatigable author seems to have produced a separate work covering both these subjects and much else besides. This is the famous *Leges Henrici Primi*.[2] With great self-restraint the author now limits his preface to a few lines culled from the preface to *Quadripartitus II*, gives us once again the coronation charter of Henry I, and embarks upon the classification of 'causes' which he had promised for his projected third book. This classification turns out to be rhetorical rather than legal, and comes from St Isidore. In c. 5, however, he gets some solid legal ideas from Ivo of Chartres, St Augustine and other sources.

These cautious approaches bring him finally to English law. He tells us of Wessex, Mercia and the Danelaw, of the county and the hundred; of causes emendable and unemendable; of pleas of the crown; of pleas of the church wherein the king has a part, and of pleas involving amercement by the king. Thus far a certain chain of association is discernible, one point leading on to another. If the author goes to the Continent for his generalities, he fetches his English law largely from *Quadripartitus I* and especially from that part of it where he was translating from Alfred or Cnut. There are fairly numerous passages, however, where the author seems to speak out of his own knowledge without relying upon

---

[1] Liebermann, *op. cit.* III, 309.

[2] Liebermann, *op. cit.* I, 547–611. The date is between 1114 and 1118. Pollock and Maitland, *History of English Law*, I, 100 do not exclude the common authorship of *Quadripartitus* and the *Leges*, but Liebermann's *Gesetze* (where the identical authorship is established) did not begin to appear until 1903, and Maitland's second edition was in 1898. Maitland accepted Liebermann's identification in his *Collected Papers*, III, 470 (from the *Quarterly Review*, 1904).

authority. These are naturally of the greatest value and deserve close attention. The spirit and quality of those remarks, indeed, show through the author's Latin, leaving us with the impression that even when he is adapting Cnut's laws he probably does so deliberately because he recognizes in them the legal authority which ought to secure them respect and obedience, and because he further regards them as being, even ninety years after their enactment, a true statement of current law. His chapter XCIII reproducing Alfred's long tariff of emendations must be read in this light also, for it is clear that the author kept constantly before his eyes the need to write a book of practical, current law.

In other words, this author was writing a text-book of his own contemporary law. At hardly any other period of our history was that so difficult and hazardous a task as in the years 1114–18. At the head of his book he rightly put the intensely feudal coronation charter of Henry I: and yet that same charter granted the '*lagam Edwardi regis*'; the old and the new social structures, the old and the new procedures were at work side by side, together with the old and the new vocabularies. In one line he tells us of 'fiefs', in the next of 'bookland'.[1] So unmanageable a conglomeration of rules and institutions would have made almost impossible demands upon the skill of a much more resourceful writer than our author. Considering his limitations, he did a useful piece of work.

What can we say of his technique of book-writing? The question is difficult, and Bishop Stubbs approached it with even more than his usual discouraging expressions of distaste at the beginning of a lecture. 'We have now come', said he, 'to the hardest, if not to the dullest and driest, perhaps also the most remunerative, part of the work which we have set ourselves, the examination of the so-called *Leges Henrici Primi*.'[2] When he comes finally to the question which we have posed, the bishop adds 'that so far as arrangement goes it is a labyrinth of difficulties, so puzzling and unsatisfactory that it would be a waste both of my time and yours to attempt a *rationale* of it. The best course, I think, will be to regard it for the most part as an undigested mass of detail.'[3] We can at least say this, that the author studied his authorities thoroughly, translating Cnut and the rest of the laws from the difficult Anglo-Saxon into his own brand of Latin in *Quadripartitus I*. The pre-eminence

[1] *Leges Henrici Primi*, LXX, 21.
[2] Stubbs, *Lectures in Early English History*, p. 143.   [3] *Ibid.* p. 150.

which he gives to Cnut is sensible, although he fully recognizes that Henry I in his coronation charter had granted the *laga Edwardi*, and he seems trying to be fair when he concludes his work with passages from both Cnut and from Alfred. His use of St Isidore and such unusual sources as the Salic and Ripuarian laws shows his search for authority into the remote and Continental past; his use of contemporary canonical sources such as the *Decretum* and the *Panormia* of Ivo of Chartres shows that he chose the most advanced of his recent contemporaries. He did indeed have the problem of arrangement forced upon his attention. In *Quadripartitus* he understandably put Cnut first as the most recent and authoritative statement of Anglo-Saxon law: but having done that, he deliberately adopted a chronological arrangement (or very nearly so) for the much older material, and translated each king's laws in the order in which he found them. It is only when we come to the *Leges Henrici* that we find him attempting one further step: he dissects the laws of the various kings and re-assembles the fragments, with his own comments and contributions to cover the joins and fill the gaps.

That question of order gave him a lot of trouble. He sought with some diligence a general scheme suitable for a law-book. Unfortunately he looked too far back in history and took for his guide St Isidore's *Etymologiae*.[1] No doubt that was the standard encyclopedia of the Middle Ages, but it was a product of the seventh century, and the passages he lighted upon were not so much legal as poor specimens of decadent rhetoric. He reproduced them carefully,[2] but manifestly they were useless. He evidently felt that he fared better when he turned to the *Decretum* and *Panormia* of Ivo of Chartres. But at the end of it all, he never succeeded in distinguishing the wood from the trees—and, as we have seen, his wood was a sadly overgrown and neglected place, his trees the noble but decaying relics of a dying age.

There is thus every excuse for the *Leges Henrici* being an untidy and disorganized book; if it had been written only one generation later, it would certainly have been much better. To his credit, our author kept on trying, and kept on learning—can anyone do more than that? Finally, he earned a handsome tribute from Maitland which may be repeated here, for it is often misquoted: 'we should

---

[1] The modern edition is by W. M. Lindsay (2 vols., Oxford, 1910).
[2] *Leges Henrici Primi*, IV.

remember that he was engaged upon an utterly new task, new in England, new in Europe; he was writing a legal text-book that was neither Roman nor Canon law. To have thought that a law-book ought to be written was no small exploit in 1118.'[1]

It was Glanvill,[2] or whoever it was who wrote the book which bears that name,[3] who found the solution to our problem of authority, and upon that solution constructed a book which is the English echo to Gratian. The echo was indeed a generation late, but, in view of what has just been said, it indicates that England was rapidly catching up with the times. Nor is the echo a mere mechanical repetition or imitation of Continental themes; there were local conditions which had to be taken into account.

A faithful imitation of the best Continental twelfth-century legal literature would have produced a very different Glanvill from the book which has come down to us. Perhaps the author of Glanvill contemplated this possibility with some care before he abandoned it. In the Continental models a large part was assigned to the papal decretals and the canons of councils—to the formal pronouncements of high authorities. Glanvill might well have followed the same course. His predecessor had already set the coronation charter of Henry I at the head of a law-book; Glanvill himself used conspicuously canonical language in what is now believed to have been the earlier version of his book:[4] and Henry II had been issuing 'assizes' which were to shape the law for centuries to come; could there be any authorities more impressive than these? Did they not deserve collection, arrangement, annotation, careful study? These assizes were solemn and deliberate acts which were published to the world at large, and the government itself took careful steps to ensure their conservation. Some abbeys received copies of these documents and transcribed at least some of them into their monastic chronicle, by which means we know of them today. Indeed, the whole of Glanvill's treatise occurs in Hoveden's Chronicle,

---

[1] Pollock and Maitland, *op. cit.* I, 100–1. It is proper to read those famous words in conjunction with Maitland's cautious warning, *ibid.* p. 167.

[2] First printed *c.* 1554; the latest edition is by G. E. Woodbine, 1932. A new edition is in preparation by R. W. Southern and G. D. G. Hall.

[3] Lady Stenton, *Pleas before the King* (Selden Society, vol. LXVII), I, 9, following R. W. Southern, suggests Geoffrey fitz Peter rather than Hubert Walter; for jokes about the archbishop's Latin, see Giraldus Cambrensis, *Opera*, II, 344; III, 254.

[4] R. W. Southern, 'Note on the text of "Glanville"', *English Historical Review*, LXV, 81.

where it appears among official documents.[1] In Glanvill's day it would have been easy to assemble the assizes of Henry II, and possibly some acts of his predecessors as well, and Hubert Walter had the true bureaucrat's instinct for amassing rolls and files.[2] Peterborough had impressive collections, and at this moment Englishmen were conspicuous in the urgent work of collecting *extravagantes*.[3] The strong royalist flavour which a collection of assizes and legislative documents would certainly have would hardly have displeased the king. Seventy years previously *Quadripartitus* had collected royalist state papers, and Glanvill might well have pursued the same policy. For some reason which we do not know, the book called 'Glanvill' did not take that form. Perhaps the assizes were not quite extensive enough to cover all the ground which the author intended to deal with; perhaps, too, the author desired to avoid the very acute political issues involved in some of these documents,[4] especially the Constitutions of Clarendon; moreover, the quarrel of Henry II and Becket had ended on a note of high tragedy which was absent from the contest of Henry I and St Anselm. Indeed, could one forget during Henry II's lifetime the heavy penance which he had to undergo at the tomb of St Thomas?

However that may have been, the momentous choice of Glanvill fell upon writs, rather than upon legislation, as his authorities. After all, he was only concerned with English law, not with universal law, and since his book was meant to be local, it was appropriate to base it upon local procedural forms. The same thought had occurred long ago to Burchard of Worms who made wide use of procedural forms in a work which was intended to be distinctly regional—so too did Regino of Prüm.

Writs were to be the authorities, therefore, around which Glanvill built his book. There immediately arose the question which he had to face, and as far as possible to settle, at the very outset: where to begin? how is the material to be arranged? As everyone knows, there are countless manuscripts called 'Registrum

---

[1] *Rogeri de Houedene Chronica*, ed. Stubbs, I, intro. pp. lxxv ff.; Pollock and Maitland, *History of English Law*, I, 163 n. 1.

[2] A. L. Poole, *Domesday Book to Magna Carta*, pp. 442–3.

[3] S. Kuttner and E. Rathbone, 'Anglo-Norman canonists of the twelfth century', *Traditio*, VII, 279, especially p. 283.

[4] It is quite clear, however, that Glanvill wholeheartedly accepts the implications of the Constitutions of Clarendon.

Brevium' containing various selections from those writs which were current in practice. The earliest specimen known to us is dated 1227;[1] its contents are older still and carry us back to within thirty years of Glanvill's treatise. Two possible solutions confront us. Either there was already in existence some collection of writs and Glanvill took it as his text or, alternatively, there was no attempt at collecting writs until Glanvill for the first time undertook it, and subsequent registers were derived from his.

To decide between these two possibilities is difficult. If the register which the government sent to Ireland for use there in 1227 was a new compilation prepared for that purpose, it is curious that it should contain writs which manifestly date from King John's reign; it seems more reasonable to suppose that it was not a new compilation, but a copy of one already in circulation and enjoying the repute of an acknowledged and reputed practitioner's book. The fact that the forms in it were at least eleven years old was not a matter of serious consequence: both in England and in Ireland lawyers would not be perturbed.

Moreover, we must beware of speaking of 'the register'. No two registers are alike save in the broadest sense. They all contain individual variants in content; even that material which appears in wellnigh all of them may not appear in the same order. In a very laborious set of articles[2] Maitland analysed a number of manuscript registers from various dates, and his results seem to indicate a slow tendency towards uniformity by the end of the Middle Ages. That is exactly the reverse of the normal development of a work which begins as the author's copy, and achieves increasing diversity as successive copyists and editors leave their mark upon it. The passage of time brought some measure of uniformity to the register, although it brought divergence to works which had begun with a single original.

In all the manuscripts which Maitland examined he found wide divergences in arrangement. It is difficult to draw any other conclusion than that registers do not derive from a single author, and that 'the register' did not imply to medieval lawyers—any

[1] Coke's claim to have a register of Henry II, i.e. of Glanvill's day or even earlier, must be attributed to his collector's enthusiasm: *Jehu Webb's Case* (1608), 8 Rep. 45 b at 47 b.

[2] 'The history of the register of original writs', *Harvard Law Review*, III, 97, 167, 212; the articles are reprinted in Maitland, *Collected Papers*, II, 110–73 and in *Select Essays in Anglo-American Legal History*, II, 549 ff.

more than to modern historians—any sort of official origin. We must go even further, and admit that the great first step of Continental lawyers—to arrange their material systematically—had hardly appeared in England. Indeed, down to the end of the story (the last printed edition appeared in 1687) there is no ascertainable scheme of arrangement in the Register.

When the 'Register' was so amorphous, it is hopeless to attempt to identify traces of it in Glanvill's treatise. Maitland's impression was that there could hardly have been anything like a register of writs before the reign of Henry II; yet he deems it possible that Glanvill may have followed the order of some already existing register. That leaves a very narrow margin of time between Glanvill and the first register; and likewise a narrow margin is observable between Glanvill and the first extant register, which although dated 1227 can be shown to be a copy of writs issued in the reign of John and consequently before 1216. This may or may not imply the existence of a collection of writs in John's day. Whether Glanvill had at his disposal a pre-existing register, and furthermore whether he in fact followed its arrangement, or whether his was the first attempt at collecting writs, is therefore an insoluble question at present. But it is certain that his method fixed in the minds of English lawyers for centuries to come the conviction that writs were the paramount *authoritates* from which proceeded the law of the land. It was clearly a practical fact; Glanvill made it a part of our legal science when he built his book around it.

It now remains to examine Glanvill's book and the organization of his material in the light of the best work of the day. He begins with a prologue which obviously derives from the *Proemium* to Justinian's *Institutes*. There follows a table of contents in one group of manuscripts; the other group has instead of it chapter headings inserted in the course of the text, which vary somewhat from manuscript to manuscript. The significance of this, and the conclusion as to what was Glanvill's original method will depend upon the view one takes of the relationship of the manuscripts— and at this point it must be confessed that serious criticisms have recently been made by Mr Southern[1] upon the text constructed by the latest editor, the late Professor Woodbine. Book I follows, but its first three chapters, occupying together less than thirty

[1] See his article in *English Historical Review*, LXV, 81.

lines of print, merit special attention. They sketch very briefly a division of proceedings into civil and criminal, royal and vice-comital. It is a very elementary attempt to lay down some of the main lines of legal analysis. The contrast with the *Leges Henrici Primi* is a measure of the intellectual, as well as of the legal, revolution accomplished during the sixty years separating the two works. Glanvill, or the author of that book, had set his face in the right direction. He did not proceed very far, but nevertheless his small page of generalities bore rich fruit: Bracton expanded it nearly three-hundred-fold.

After that slight but significant gesture, Glanvill gets down to work. As in all the registers of writs, and all the institutional works based upon them (except Bracton), the first topic is the writ of right. Maitland long ago noted that the faint ghost of a plan uniting the registers consists in beginning with right and concluding with possession. That plan is discernible in Glanvill, but with a difference. The common arrangement was to begin with the writ of right *de recto* which began in the lord's feudal court; Glanvill, however, began with the writ of right *precipe quod reddat* which began in the king's court. Not until Book XII (and there are only fourteen books altogether) does he deal with the writ of right *de recto*. This is a remarkable peculiarity. Our early registers and the instructional books derived from them begin with the writ of right *de recto* in various forms and for various sorts of tenement, and proceed only much later to the *precipe quod reddat*, and for very good reasons. The substantive law is the same. Procedure is indeed vastly different in the early stages, but, if ever the writ *de recto* gets into the king's court by means of *tolt* and *pone*, it then becomes indistinguishable from a *precipe quod reddat*. Bracton treats the two concurrently.

It seems at first sight, therefore, that Glanvill missed an obvious opportunity for systematization when he put the writ *precipe quod reddat* in his Book I, and deferred the writ of right *de recto* until Book XII, almost at the end of his work. He also succeeded in mystifying Maitland—and there we are clearly warned to proceed with caution. In the course of the famous articles to which allusion has already been made, Maitland took Glanvill as our earliest collection of writs, and compared his collection with that in the Irish register of 1227 and in a Cambridge manuscript (Ii. vi. 13) of very nearly the same date. Putting these texts in chronological order, with Glanvill coming first, Maitland at once observed that Glanvill began with the *precipe quod reddat* although the Irish and other registers begin instead with the *de recto* form of the writ of right. 'This was a victory of feudalism consecrated by the Great Charter.' It was indeed tempting to regard the sturdy royalism of Glanvill as being ousted by the 'feudalism' of the registers which succeeded it, with the writ of right *de recto* in the place of honour, and Magna Carta consecrating the victory of feudalism. In fact, however, we have no need to interpret events in terms of such great themes as Monarchy *v.* Feudalism, for the title of Glanvill's treatise makes it perfectly plain that 'it contains only those laws and customs according to which there is pleading in the king's court, at the exchequer, and before justices wherever they be'. It matters little for our purpose whether that title was written by the author himself or by someone else—in either case it is a precise and accurate description of the aim and content of the treatise, which is concerned with proceedings in the king's courts and nowhere else. Once this point is clear, the rest inevitably follows and the *precipe quod reddat* must necessarily be chosen as the writ of right since the writ is issued to the king's sheriff in the first place, and all the proceedings upon it take place in the royal court. On the other hand, the writ of right *de recto* begins in a seignorial court and will continue there until it is removed into the king's court on the ground (real or supposed) of failure of justice, or is subsequently attacked in the king's court for 'false judgement'. It is the possibility of writs coming to the king's court *per translationem* which is the principal subject of Glanvill's Book XII, and it is in that book that we duly find the writs *de recto*.

Glanvill put some of his writs of right at the beginning of his treatise, and others very near the end; but he had good reasons, for he was writing only of law and practice in the king's court. His primary duty was therefore to deal with writs in the form *precipe quod reddat* because their whole course was passed in the royal jurisdictions: of writs *de recto* he had to deal only in so far as they might at some stage be removed into the royal court. Many no doubt were, but an unascertainably large number were satisfactorily disposed of in the seignorial courts without ever coming before the royal justices. The wide separation of these two classes of writ is therefore perfectly logical and explicable without recourse to the dramatic interpretation suggested by Maitland.

In some other respects also Glanvill made progess in classifying writs of right; where the *Leges Henrici Primi* seems only directed by a vague sort of association of ideas, one point leading to another, Glanvill seems moved by genuine scientific motives when he put his writs together. Thus he made the writ of right of advowson follow immediately upon the writ of right *precipe quod reddat* for land and resisted the temptation (which seduced some later authors) of being diverted either into the petty assizes or into darrein presentment. Nor does he put the writ of right of dower among his first group (for it is brought in the lord's court and not in the king's); instead he proceeds to the apparently unrelated subject of naifty—for the perfectly logical reason that it may be in the nature of a writ of right which must be brought in the royal court if the alleged villein offers to prove his liberty—as the king explains to the sheriff in his writ *de libertate probanda*: 'it belongs not to you to take that kind of proof'. He has made a choice and bases his classification upon the nature of the proceedings instead of upon the nature of the thing sought by those proceedings—land, an advowson, a villein or the like. That choice, we must insist, is based upon the author's theory of law and his conception of the underlying unity which brings together in one category all those actions which later theorists were to call *droiturel*, and not upon the more obvious, but superficial, distinctions which would immediately strike a layman between land, an advowson and a man. As we have seen, the author of *Leges Henrici Primi* let himself be carried away by the rhetoricians when he looked to St Isidore for some hints on classification: the author of Glanvill is on surer ground and realized that the arrangement of his treatise was dictated by essentially legal considerations of the sort of remedy sought, and the nature of the proceedings used. There is no fumbling or hesitation; we are, for the first time in the history of our law, presented with a law-book, written by a lawyer, framed upon principles derived from the law, and not from those of any other science.

At this point, therefore, English law becomes autonomous. Its independence was strikingly illustrated by the appearance at almost the same time of the *Dialogus de Scaccario*[1] which was devoted mainly to administration: so too a little earlier, canon law and theology found separate treatment in the works of Peter

[1] Text and translation by Charles Johnson (Edinburgh, 1950).

Lombard and Gratian. No doubt our Glanvill was hardly conscious of the implications of all this, but patiently pursued his way, methodically and logically, applying not so much the text as the spirit of the best Continental work accessible to him. Having done with villeinage, he brings us, in his Book VI, to dower, which he introduces with the explanation that *dos* in this country means what common lawyers call 'dower'—and in book VII he will explain in due course that *dos* in the Roman sense is called *maritagium* in England. The treatment of dower in Book VI begins with an exceptionally long introduction in dialectical style before coming to the texts of the writs: Book VII is still more expository in style, and also miscellaneous in content, for it seems to deal with all those questions which may arise when there has been a death in the family. Here the author is not quite so sure of his method. Thus a passage on *maritagia* leads to 'gifts' generally, and the limits of alienability. Since a donor 'and his heirs' are generally bound by the terms of the usual form of gift to warrant, the author next defines 'heirs' and then proceeds to wills, wardships, bastardy and escheat. Finally a fuller treatment of *maritagia* concludes the book. Glanvill's Book VII is therefore of exceptional interest, both for its content and its method. Lengthy as it is, it contains but two writs, and those of minor consequence. The author of Glanvill, like the author of the *Leges Henrici Primi*, is at his most illuminating when he has no authorities to follow: reading Glanvill's treatise as a whole, one cannot fail to be struck by the clarity of the exposition when the author cuts adrift from his procedural authorities, and to wonder why he so radically changed his method at this point.

If we can only guess the reason, we can nevertheless guess with a certain degree of probability. The great revolution in the common law which brought primogeniture and freedom of alienation was taking place at this very moment. Glanvill had to admit that many points were disputable in the king's court, and that in others it could proceed *ex aequitate* rather than by law.[1] As for forms, it is most unlikely that in this field they had as yet been sufficiently settled for him to be able to use them as authorities. It must have been a bewildering situation, but we must acknowledge with respectful admiration how brilliantly Glanvill acquitted himself. He saw clearly the points in debate and explained them lucidly.

[1] Cf. Hazeltine, 'Judicial discretion in English procedure of Henry the Second's time', *Festschrift Gierke*, p. 1055.

He firmly turned his eyes away from the past, and in effect laid down the law of the future. Only two generations ago his predecessor had been wrestling with the laws of Alfred and Cnut and Ethelred, and Glanvill's own contemporaries were at the very moment still painfully copying out the *Leges Henrici Primi* and *Quadripartitus* in dozens of manuscripts. Glanvill was above all the sentimental talk about the *laga Edwardi* and wrote—consciously and deliberately it must have been—the law of the future. Written in a moment of supreme crisis in our legal history, before there were as yet any authoritative documents to guide him, the courage and mastery which produced Glanvill's Book VII are unsurpassed in our legal history.

Book VIII on fines is full of forms and writs; Book IX on homage, relief and purpresture has a long preliminary dissertation. Book X begins with debt and then proceeds with sureties, to conclude with gage and mortgage and the sale of goods. The very short Book XI tells us a little about the *responsalis* who represents his principal in litigation.

All that has been mentioned thus far falls within the first grand division of Glanvill's book, that is to say, pleas which begin in the king's court. Book XII introduces a new subject—those pleas which only reach the king's court *per translationem* from some other tribunal in which they originated. It begins with the writ of right *de recto* for various types of hereditament, and briefly explains the jurisdiction of the sheriff, but he says it is really outside his main subject, which is the king's court only. So Book XIII brings us back to the royal jurisdiction with those intensely royal remedies, the petty assizes. The brief Book XIV concludes the whole work with a few remarks about crime.

From the large number of manuscripts still surviving, it is obvious that Glanvill was much used, and for about a century after it was written. At least three manuscripts exist which are not in Latin but in French,[1] which probably means that the book was found useful for the business man as well as for the lawyer; and at least two versions are known in which attempts were made to modernize his text, one about 1250[2] and the other about

---

[1] British Museum, Lansd. 467; Cambridge University Library, Ee. i. 1; Ll. i. 16.

[2] British Museum, Harl. 323; Add. 25005; H. G. Richardson, 'Glanville continued', *Law Quarterly Review*, LIV, 381.

1263.[1] The first part of the *Très Ancien Coutumier* of Normandy which dates from the early years of King John (1199–1204) presents its material in an order which recalls that of Glanvill, and the influence of Glanvill upon the *Regiam Majestatem* has long been a teasing problem in the legal history of Scotland.[2]

The theme of this discourse has been the gradual emergence of principle in our law. At first this is merely a matter of literary presentation—the discovery of the trick of writing a systematic law-book. Ultimately the new form was destined to mould the substance of the law as well, making it a rational science instead of a merely pious observance of antique rituals. That development, it must be remembered, was very long and had been in progress all through the Anglo-Saxon period. It had always been the business of the monarchy, advised and encouraged by the church, to reform the traditional law upon rational lines, and all through Anglo-Saxon legal history there are traces of reform, rationality and discretion in the laws themselves which may escape the notice of a hurried reader. The efforts of the Roman Church to curb the extravagances of the Celtic penitentials are a parallel phenomenon in a different field. But these are all matters of detail. To see law as an articulated whole and to present its details as a series of corollaries to a few master-theorems was an intellectual adventure which had not yet begun. It took nigh a thousand years for Roman law to discover the road, and to take some significant steps along it. To the eager band of legists, who found the net results of that development in the books of Justinian, it seemed that they had received a precious revelation, and indeed so they had. To the canonists the problem was rather different. They shared with the theologians a still greater revelation which was guarded not by an extinct state, but by a living church. The *Corpus Juris Civilis* had been completed long ago; the *Corpus Juris Canonici* still remained to be written, from materials which came not from a dead Augustus but from a vigorous papacy which was daily adding to their mass in canons and decretals.

A total reception of Roman results was as impossible to the canonist as a total reception of Aristotle was to the theologian. Both faculties were faced with the same problem and both solved

[1] Cambridge University Library, Mm. i. 27; F. W. Maitland, 'Glanville revised', *Collected Papers*, II, 266.
[2] See H. G. Richardson in *Juridical Review*, LXVII, 155.

it the same way. The ancients had indeed provided an immensely rich heritage of law and philosophy which medieval thinkers accepted with gratitude and reverence; but they realized (quite unconsciously, no doubt) that their task was not to find safe investments for an inherited fortune, but to start from the beginning and create a new one. Indeed, the passage of the centuries had gravely dilapidated the legacies of Greece and Rome. The two surviving productive assets were first, the inspiring memory of great things done, and secondly, the great gift of a method. Encouraged by the one, and armed with the other, the Middle Ages set out afresh upon its own new adventure.

Englishmen took part in these great events. In theology and philosophy they were conspicuous in the front rank. In canon and civil law they produced competent subalterns: perhaps to a man with a legal cast of mind the situation in domestic English law offered more interesting work and rewards nearer home. And yet, even within the narrow boundaries of a local system of lay law, there were men in England who started a new movement which was to sweep over Europe and produce a new set of major problems. The unknown author of the *Leges Henrici Primi* was the first anywhere to envisage a book primarily devoted to a body of territorial law which was neither canon nor Roman. He suffered from many handicaps. His early education had obviously been neglected; but he had read the best recent work of the Continent and had Ivo of Chartres at his elbow. Moreover, he wrote at a great crisis of English law, and clung to a losing cause—the laws of Cnut (which is rather odd, for he was plainly of French ancestry). All the same he wrote and rewrote his books, clumsily but sincerely. Two generations later another anonymous writer produced a very different book, conspicuously confined to the lay courts. The quality of his contribution can hardly be overestimated. Where Gratian had perfected the method slowly evolved by fifty predecessors, Glanvill sprang fully armed from the practice of the king's court. Ruthlessly he jettisoned the laws of Henry I, of Cnut, of Alfred and all the rest of our ancients. He accepted, like Gratian, the Continental plan of building his book around authorities, linked together with comment; but his authorities were not canons nor decretals nor their English equivalents, but writs.

That choice was momentous. It fixed in the minds of all subsequent lawyers the conviction that writs were the backbone of

English law. It also placed a gulf between English and Continental law. Neither of these two conclusions was willingly accepted. A generation after Glanvill, people were still ready to welcome books which purported to be the laws of Edward the Confessor or the forest ordinances of King Cnut. To others, such as William of Longchamp[1] who wrote contemporaneously with Glanvill, it seemed more promising to abandon the past and to try to write a treatise which should combine in some way English, Roman and canonical procedure. Later still, Bracton continued the belief that light could be found in the comparative method. Time was to prove that Glanvill was right. The preoccupation of some writers with the Anglo-Saxon laws could lead to nothing but a barren and dishonest romanticism—with the *Mirror of Justices* at the end of the road. The concern of others with Roman and canon law could contribute a valuable intellectual stimulus, but could contribute nothing else, to the practical framework of English common law. 'Pierre de Fontaines in the Vermandois could romanize without the restraint of a *Registrum Brevium*', so Maitland long ago remarked,[2] but the position of England by the end of the twelfth century had already become clear: as Glanvill had perceived, English law was the law of writs.

[1] His *Practica Legum et Decretorum* is printed in E. Caillemer, *Droit civil dans les provinces anglo-normandes*; P. Vinogradoff, *Roman Law in Mediaeval Europe* (ed de Zulueta), p. 100.
[2] *Bracton and Azo* (Selden Society, vol. VIII), p. xxxi.

CHAPTER III

BRACTON AND HIS WORK

ONE of the pleasantest academic pastimes is that called 'textual criticism'. In its simplest form it requires little apparatus and demands no lengthy or fatiguing effort. All it needs is a text with a few teasing obscurities, and a critic with a sound knowledge of the language commanded by a nimble and ingenious mind. The rest could be left to the inspired guess or the happy intuition of the critic. For a long time the game was controlled by learned amateurs, some of whom came very near genius. Such was the great Richard Bentley (1662–1742),[1] Master of Trinity, who set the standards not only for Cambridge and England, but for the whole learned world besides. Even in his day, however, textual criticism was a rough game, and its practice for over a century afterwards engendered fierce controversy, as the *Letters of Phalaris* (1695) were succeeded by the poems of *Ossian* (1762), the *Rowley Poems* (1777), the play *Vortigern* (1786) and Ireland's *Text of Shakespeare* (1852). The emendation of genuine texts and the falsification (and subsequent exposure) of supposititious works afforded immense excitement as textual criticism transcended the bounds of a select group of university scholars and became the entertainment of the growing class of readers in the world of letters. Bentley was doing his best work in the reign of Queen Anne, but a century later the situation had changed. Learned Germans elaborated and professionalized critical methods, invented new techniques, and endeavoured to make them into a new science.[2]

For several generations our own Bracton has been subjected to ceaseless fire from the heaviest of these modern weapons, and from time to time it is desirable to try and find out how he has fared. This

---

[1] See the excellent little book on *Bentley* contributed to the 'English Men of Letters' series by Sir Richard Jebb.

[2] For short introductions, see N. Denholm-Young in *Chambers' Encyclopedia of Literature* (ed. S. H. Steinberg), I, 542–6 and the older papers of J. P. Postgate in the *Encyclopedia Britannica* (11th ed.), XXVI, 708–15; L. Havet, *Manuel de critique verbale appliquée aux textes latins* (1911); W. W. Greg, *The Calculus of Variants* (Oxford, 1927); J. Destrez, *La Pecia* (Paris, 1935), especially pp. 63 ff.; J. P. Postgate's article in J. E. Sandys, *Companion to Latin Studies*, pp. 791–805; E. W. Hall, *Companion to Classical Texts* (1913); cf. below, p. 53.

is not without peril, however, for there is always the risk of getting caught in the fire of zealous colleagues. As things are comparatively quiet for the moment this may be a suitable time for a cautious reconnaissance of the Bractonian position.

For the first time in this survey we are able to ascribe with confidence a name and an identity to the author of an English law-book. The first printed edition has familiarized us with the form 'Bracton', but it is clear that in the Middle Ages it was 'Bratton' for the places and for the man. For his life, as for the lives of so many medieval worthies, we have in the records an abundance of insignificant detail, but hardly anything which indicates the distinctive characteristics or the personality of the author.

We learn that Bracton began to draw a salary of forty marks a year from the exchequer in 1240,[1] which may reasonably imply that he had entered the royal service one year before in 1239. In what capacity he served we are not told—possibly as one of those trusted clerks who were not permanently attached to any particular department but could be assigned to special duties as occasion required. In 1242–3 we casually learn that he held a knight's fee in Alverdiscott of Baldwin the Fleming, who held of Richard earl of Cornwall, brother of Henry III.[2] It is notable that Bracton twice contrives to mention Richard of Cornwall conspicuously in the course of his book.[3] This feudal connexion may well have played a part in bringing Bracton into touch with the court. Moreover, it seems almost certainly an inheritance rather than a gift or a purchase.

If Bracton's land-tenure in 1242–3 indicates one sort of connexion, we learn of another from a document of 1245 which at first sight shows him to have been as well launched in ecclesiastical circles as he was in feudal standing and in administrative affairs. William Rayleigh, bishop of Winchester, had a power delegated from the pope to dispense any two of his clerks from the canons against pluralism. He exercised this power in 1245 in favour (a) of Geoffrey of Ferring, who was his official and eventually became dean of St Paul's, and (b) of Henry of Bracton, who is described as rector of Gosberton in the diocese of Lincoln. This

---

[1] *Calendar of Liberate Rolls, 1226–1240*, p. 450.
[2] *Book of Fees*, II, 795; Round, 'Bractoniana', *English Historical Review*, XXXI, 586.　　　　[3] Bracton, f. 47, f. 382 b.

document of 1245 is a papal confirmation of the bishop's use of his powers in favour of Ferring and Bracton.[1] One immediately wonders how a Lincolnshire rector could be described as a 'clerk' of the bishop of Winchester. Geoffrey of Ferring was indeed the bishop's official (which means that he presided in the bishop's episcopal court). Ought we to ascribe to Bracton some unnamed dignity which would justify Rayleigh in calling Bracton his 'clerk'? If we could that would account for the privilege, and also account for Bracton's knowledge of Roman and canon law. Unfortunately there are no episcopal registers for Winchester until 1282.

It seems clear that we must abandon the idea that Bracton was Rayleigh's 'clerk' in the ecclesiastical sense, with its implication that Bracton was either beneficed, or dignified, or in some other way under Rayleigh's episcopal jurisdiction. But he could have been Rayleigh's clerk in the vaguer and more worldly sense of the word, as being his personal employee attending his master in some of the multifarious duties which fell upon him. It is not easy to believe that Bracton was engaged either in an academic career, or in the sort of ecclesiastical career which his fellow-beneficiary Geoffrey of Ferring had pursued. Nor do such signal dispensations as Rayleigh conferred upon his two 'clerks' come the way of a simple country parson—which is all that Bracton seems to have been, ecclesiastically speaking, in 1245. It seems more likely that Bracton got his rectory, and his dispensation, in the same way as Rayleigh got his bishopric, by service to the king; for Rayleigh had spent many years on the bench as a royal judge.

This raises a great many important questions. In the first place forty marks per annum in 1240 meant the substantial salary of a senior man who had achieved a position of dignity and responsibility in the public service. It was not a commencing salary; on the contrary it is well up towards the top of the scale. It would be unwarranted to conclude that because Bracton first appears on the Liberate roll in 1240 his working life for the king began in that year. It would be more consonant with medieval practice if we were to assume that he had spent some years as a trainee (so to speak) without salary, although not necessarily without reward in the shape of his rectory, dining rights, livery of robes and similar small favours. It is in the years before 1240 that Bracton had the

---

[1] *Calendar of Papal Letters*, I, 220–1.

hard uphill task of making a place for himself either in church, or state, or both. Bishop Rayleigh's grant of privilege suggests at first sight that Bracton had his feet on the ecclesiastical ladder; but his forty marks a year shows that he was already equally well advanced up the civil service hierarchy. The fact that his salary was raised later to fifty pounds a year[1] shows that he was unmistakably getting on in the royal service.

The key to these puzzles is surely Rayleigh himself. In his book Bracton has two judicial heroes, Martin Pateshall (who died in 1229 when Bracton could hardly have advanced far, if at all, in his career), and William Rayleigh. For these two royal judges he had profound respect and warm admiration, which both of them deserved. Pateshall 'is nearly the first, if not the very first Englishman who becomes famous as a learned industrious judge and no more'.[2] Rayleigh, who lived until 1250, had been 'the premier judge, travelling about with the king and hearing those pleas which followed the king'.[3] Already in 1234 he delivered the great judgment reversing the outlawry of Hubert de Burgh which is one of the most impressive vindications of the rule of law in our history.[4] But Bracton mentions none of his own colleagues—Preston, Thurkelby, Bath, Lexington—for their exploits, which were notable, we must depend upon those small tracts which we shall have to consider in a later chapter.[5]

Why this devotion to Rayleigh? Maitland mentioned, but declined to stress the similarity of constitutional outlook which Rayleigh and Bracton shared. To him it seemed 'mere chance' that Bracton got hold of Rayleigh's rolls and not those of some other judge such as Segrave. Or, more probably (he surmised), Bracton may have regarded Rayleigh as head of a 'school' of legal thought. Again, when Bracton visited Devonshire, he chose a Rayleigh to sit with him on the bench; and in later life he held lands of the Rayleighs. These facts, though true, we must postpone (for in any case they belong to a later stage of his career) and stick to our immediate question of how and why Bracton obtained such signal favour from Rayleigh at the early date of 1245 (a fact, by the way, which Maitland barely mentioned). Finally, Maitland concluded

---

[1] *Calendar of Patent Rolls, 1247–1258*, p. 450.
[2] Maitland, in *Bracton's Note Book*, I, 45.
[3] *Ibid.* I, 46.　　　　　　　　　　[4] *Bracton's Note Book*, no. 857.
[5] Those tracts, however, although they mention Bracton's contemporaries, do not mention Rayleigh.

a page of conjecture with the words 'possibly he was the pupil, the clerk, the friend of Bishop William'.[1]

This last suggestion, which Maitland did not develop, has proved the most attractive to later writers (except to Mr Richardson).[2] It is well established that some judges' clerks have risen to the bench, and it is equally clear that such clerks might not appear on the royal payrolls, since they were the personal employees of the judges. On the other hand, a man who was already a king's clerk might be occasionally detailed to act as a clerk of an eyre. There was no regular establishment to confine such men, and we cannot safely draw inferences. The hard core of fact with which we must deal is that in 1245 Bishop Rayleigh conferred the valuable though unseemly privilege of holding in plurality three benefices with cure of souls upon his 'clerk' Henry of Bracton, rector of Gosberton in the diocese of Lincoln. If Bracton had been the rising canonist which Mr Richardson has suggested, he would surely have held some ecclesiastical office comparable to that held by his fellow-beneficiary Ferring; to confer such a valuable privilege upon a simple rector, beneficed moreover in another diocese, may well seem curious. It seems inescapable that Bracton's claim upon the bishop's bounty was not ecclesiastical, but lay, and that Bracton had been Rayleigh's clerk in the worldly sense of the word before he became the 'king's clerk' in 1239.

There is another curious circumstance which needs explanation. It would be perfectly normal for Rayleigh to push the fortunes of one of his promising young men; but why should he have given his dispensation to someone who had been in an established post with the king for some five or six years? The king's forty marks a year was sufficient to secure the exclusive services of almost any able young man in the land; why should Rayleigh (who has only two dispensations in his gift) bestow one of them upon Bracton, the king's clerk? Is it not for the king to look after his own?

Once again, Rayleigh is the clue. After many years' service as a judge, he left that sort of work in 1239, evidently deeming that he had earned a bishopric. Besides his own future, he had a thought for that of his clerk, Bracton. He saw that he was well provided for. Early in this very year, 1239, Bracton became an

---

[1] Maitland, *Bracton's Note Book*, I, 51, 52.
[2] Richardson, 'Azo, Drogheda and Bracton', *English Historical Review*, LIX, 27 ff.

established king's clerk and drew his first year's salary in 1240. That Bracton's devotion to Rayleigh was boundless is written on almost every page of his book: it was most appropriate that the king should take over so able and loyal a servant whose master was about to retire. Rayleigh had been active for many years, not merely as a judge of the Bench and as a judge *coram rege*, but also in much other government business; manifestly his confidential clerk was well acquainted with these state affairs. If Bracton had been a 'trainee' of some sort before he became an established king's clerk, it could only have been while he served in Rayleigh's suite. Rayleigh's retirement and Bracton's royal appointment at the same moment, when read in the light of the young man's devotion to his master, make an entirely convincing story.

Then there came a crisis in Rayleigh's affairs. He wanted a bishopric to retire to; he was elected to the see of Lichfield in February 1239, and to that of Norwich in April next. He was consecrated to Norwich. Matthew Paris[1] draws a moving picture of the angels in heaven rejoicing at the repentance of the hard-bitten lawyer-financier-politician. Those rejoicings were at least premature. Rayleigh wanted the biggest prize in England—the opulent see of Winchester. In 1242 he got it. Henry III was furious, for he had meant it for one of his wife's insatiable Savoyards. Rayleigh was driven into exile and only in 1244 was it safe for him to come back. Peace was made with the king, but Rayleigh was hopelessly impoverished by the expenses of the struggle. All the same, he gave Bracton one of his two dispensations in 1245.

Again we must ask, why did he do that? Evidently in consideration of faithful service in the years before 1239 when he could obviously have called Bracton his 'clerk'; probably, too, as an acknowledgement of more recent service. During the fierce feud with the king Rayleigh almost certainly must have used the good offices of his old servant, who was now the king's, and who could speak with the more effect since he was not yet involved in the tangled personal politics of Henry III's court. It would be very surprising if it could be shown that Bracton had no hand in bringing about the reconciliation of the king and Rayleigh.

All this bears directly on a major problem. Bracton wrote a book which displays a complete mastery of English law, and a fair acquaintance with Roman law. There are two possibilities.

---

[1] Matthew Paris, *Chronica Majora*, III, 617–18.

First, Bracton may have been a Romanist or canonist who later became immersed in the common law. That is Mr Richardson's view. Consequently, Bracton's early training must be accounted for by the surmise that he studied, and indeed taught, at Oxford. The objections to that reconstruction seem to be that Bracton's Roman law (in the opinion of most scholars) is just not good enough. He never incepted at Oxford and so his academic record (if indeed he had one at all) is too slight to explain his permanent appointment as king's clerk in 1239. On the other hand, his mastery of common law is so impressive that it is hard to believe that he acquired it hurriedly. There was no book of common law save Glanvill; having read that small tract nothing remained but practice as a means of learning English law.

The *second* possibility is that Bracton had never meant to be an academic lawyer, whether Roman or canon. Instead, he soon became connected with Rayleigh and spent his early years at Rayleigh's feet, absorbing doubtless much miscellaneous knowledge, but principally English common law. He was thus qualified for the king's service by years of experience in the period up to 1239, and had acquired claims on Rayleigh's gratitude as well.

That does not mean that he was ignorant of Roman or canon law. It must be remembered that every person in the land was subject to both the royal and canonical systems, and that even at the lowest level a knowledge of both was desirable; indeed, Mr Richardson has printed an interesting little manual of procedure dating from about 1245 wherein both canon and common law procedure are simply explained.[1] Bracton had acquired much more learning than that; but we have no need to send him to Oxford to get it. Books abounded, and Bracton's foreign law looks unmistakably bookish when compared with his treatment of common law which he had practised (as it is here suggested) in one way or another all his working life.

From the man we must turn to the book. The first impression is the bulk of it; if my estimate is correct, Bracton's treatise is about ten times the length of Glanvill's. That figure would by itself suggest the immense advance made by English law and scholarship in two generations. But if we are to examine the treatise further, we must beware. The conditions of bookmaking in the Middle

---

[1] Richardson, *Select Proceedings without Writ* (Selden Society, vol. LX), pp. cxcv–cciii: 'Consuetudines Diversarum Curiarum.'

Ages, and the hazards through which a medieval text may pass in the course of its transmission to our own day, create numerous and difficult problems. Beneath the tidy printed page there lies a situation which must be thoroughly understood before the reader can proceed further with the study of the text. These questions have been treated with great skill and patience by the late Professor Woodbine in the introductory volume to his edition.[1]

To take some examples. There is first of all the arrangement and subdivisions of the work—a matter which, we have seen, is of considerable significance in the development of English legal science. The sequence of matter from the beginning to the end of the book is the same in nearly all the manuscripts (although the large section on dower is sometimes displaced). Wide variations, however, occur in the division of the matter into books and other subdivisions. On his first page Bracton tells us that he will write his *Summa* under titles and paragraphs, but without prejudice to any better opinion. Perhaps he did so, but the manuscripts which have come down to us show neither 'titles' nor 'paragraphs' but 'books' and 'chapters'—how many books, how many chapters, and where they were to begin and end varies considerably from manuscript to manuscript. It is difficult to avoid the conclusion that Bracton's own scheme (which he sets out in very diffident language) did not commend itself to most of his readers, and so they made their own divisions.

The normal order of the great majority of the manuscripts shows with perfect clarity the scheme which Bracton was working to. The whole composition is in three very unequal portions devoted respectively to persons, things and actions. Of these, the *first* (after a few generalities about law and justice) has little to say about persons; seven folios suffice for the English equivalent of Book I of the *Institutes*, for we had little to put beside *patria potestas*, tutors and curators.

The *second* division (ff. 7b–98) on things corresponds to the second book of the *Institutes*. Both begin with the various classifications of things, and both devote much of their space to the

---

[1] Bracton was first printed in 1569, and again in 1640. The edition by Twiss in 6 vols., Rolls Series, 1878–83, has a translation and some identifications of sources, but text and translation must be used with great caution. The edition by G. E. Woodbine, 4 vols., New Haven, Conn., 1915, has an introduction in vol. I, and the complete text in vols. 2–4. The Selden Society propose to reissue Woodbine's text and add a translation, etc.

acquisition of things. Bracton did not consider himself rigidly bound, however, for he includes in this part some matters which occur in Book III of the *Institutes* (inheritance, sale), and omits testaments (of which English law had nothing to say).[1] Only a few pages, moreover, serve for the law of obligations, which in the *Institutes* forms a long transition between things and actions, but Bracton uses such material as he has for an introduction to his treatment of actions.

The *third* division (actions) comprises the last three-quarters of Bracton's work, and thus contrasts with the *Institutes* which deal with actions only in the last portion of Book IV.

At last, English legal literature had adopted a general ground-plan for a law-book. That Bracton intended the topics to succeed one another in that order is abundantly proved by the passages collected by Woodbine from the text of the treatise where Bracton says in effect 'having discussed that we now pass on to this'. Consequently the discrepancies of the manuscripts in the matter of books and chapters are of minor importance; we know what Bracton's scheme was. That scheme is clearly the order which Bracton intended; but it does not follow that he wrote the book in that order. He may well have referred back to a section which as yet only existed in his mind.

But it was a foreign scheme, and it is instructive to observe how its proportions are disturbed when it is applied to English law. We notice, for example, how scanty and how foreign is his treatment of obligations, although the *Institutes* devote considerable space to the subject; on the other hand, the inordinate bulk of the law of actions—three-quarters of the whole work—creates a monstrous distortion. If we look back for a moment to the author of Glanvill, and imagine him comparing his book with the *Institutes*, he would surely have defended himself on some such lines as these: 'Yes, I know that my little tract deals with actions and nothing else; but what else is there? I must stick to my authorities, and the only authorities in English law are the writs which entitle a court to hear this or that action.' Such a defence would be sound, and we must agree that Glanvill did as much as could then be done when he limited his work to a treatise, in effect, upon actions.

[1] Two generations previously, Glanvill (VII, 1) could still speak of a will of land, and could give a writ which seems to call upon a sheriff to enforce a reasonable 'devise' of chattels made to a house of Hospitallers; Glanvill, XII, 17.

It is equally true that Bracton could do nothing to prevent the still inordinate size of his section on actions. As a legal system develops more and more matter gets transferred from the law of actions to the law of obligations or of things until, finally, actions are reduced to the comparatively modest place accorded them in the *Institutes*. Bracton, unlike Glanvill, witnessed the beginning of that process and did all he could to further it—as Maitland and Woodbine have shown, he lavished all his skill and erudition upon the law of things.

Indeed, the first section on persons is so exiguous, that it would seem on a hasty examination that Bracton's scheme really involves two parts instead of three: first, the acquistion of property, and secondly, the law of actions. This is a fact which was bound to have some influence as Bracton became more and more aware of the shape which his book was taking. The influence is fairly clear when in the later portions of his book he gives cross-references to his section upon things. For example, he begins his discussion of dower on f. 296 with these words:

We have already spoken above of acquiring property in things and of the 'causes' thereof, and how things are acquired by reason of dower, and how dower is constituted, and how it is assigned to a woman after her husband's death, and of what things it may be had, and of what things not—all this when dower is delivered without a contest. We now come to the case where dower must be recovered by action.

The cross-reference in fact sends us to f. 92 where all these matters are duly treated, but treated in the briefest and most dogmatic language. It is evident that Bracton has been led by his scheme of arrangement to separate sharply law from procedure.[1] No surer sign of legal maturity can be adduced than this ability to see through and beyond the details of procedure so as to discern the law as a series of principles. That stage (as we have already seen) is not merely an incident in legal history; it is a fundamental step in the history of abstract thought. Theologians, canonists, civilians—all had to struggle over this *pons asinorum* before they could achieve systematic and scientific study of their material.

Bracton did this, and he did it as an integral part of his plan. Consequently, high importance attaches to the first hundred or

---

[1] The Year Books are strikingly un-Bractonian in their constant refusal to admit this separation.

so folios. It has been tempting in the past to regard them as a preliminary display of virtuosity, or as an ostentatious introduction, in romanesque language, to the main body of the work, which is pure English law. A close study of Bracton *as a whole* (and that is the chief need at the present moment) shows on the contrary that the first quarter of the book is neither irrelevant, nor detachable, nor adventitious; still less is it an impertinent attempt to impose upon the reader by 'passing off' scraps of Roman law as if they were English. If Bracton's plan is seen as a whole, it becomes clear that these early pages are an attempt to state the principles, or the general part, of our law, as a complement to the dense mass of procedure which occupies the remaining three-quarters of the book. It is there for a serious purpose, and we shall misjudge Bracton, and misunderstand his book, if we regard that section as unrelated, or as contradictory, to the rest.

That seems to be the most important aspect of the first quarter of the book. Of much more subordinate interest (although deeply fascinating, no doubt) is the use made by Bracton in that section of Roman and canon law. This question has been debated for some centuries—ever since the days of John Selden in fact.[1] It is no longer necessary to dramatize it. There was no doubt great pressure in various parts of Europe to abandon such customs as were hopelessly antiquated, and to replace them by rules of Roman or canon origin. There was likewise a strong temptation for private adventurers in the field of legal authorship to romanize their local law in order to make it more elegant from a literary point of view. In either of these two cases the result was to announce (officially or privately) that the local law contained rules which in fact it did not. That might not be as hazardous as it sounds if the local courts had already got into the habit of recruiting university-bred men as judges or advocates. In any case, that was not the position in England at the time of Bracton, and there is no evidence of imminent danger to the common law.

The problem of Bracton's romanism is thus no longer a question of life or death for the common law; but on the lower plane of a purely literary question it is one of the most fascinating problems in English legal history.

Bracton does not usually cite by name the authors he uses, but a good many of them have been by now detected: the *Institutes* of

[1] His *Dissertatio ad Fletam* first broached the subject.

Justinian obviously, but the *Digest* and the *Code* only occasionally if at all; but he uses the gloss of Accursius to the *Corpus Juris Civilis*, together with Gratian and the gloss of Johannes Teutonicus. The belief of Maitland that he used Bernard of Pavia and Tancred on marriage must now yield to the view that he used Raymond of Pennaforte (who had borrowed heavily from the two earlier authors). Then there were John de Sacrobosco (which may be translated either Hollywood or Halifax), Rogerius, John of Salisbury, Cassiodorus, the Dialogue between Solomon and Marculf[1]—and who knows how much else besides? But more than all these, which he consulted on special points, there were the two standard text-books by Azo, a *Summa* of the *Institutes* and a *Summa* of the *Code*, both written before 1211. These he must have kept at his elbow.

Rather against his will, Maitland[2] came to the conclusion that Bracton did not really understand these books, that he made egregious blunders, that he had never studied Roman law as it was studied at a university, that he was self-educated in that system, and that he remained to the end 'an uninstructed Romanist'. He had tried to pick up some Roman law out of books, and was completely out of his depth. In effect, he did not know what he was talking about.

More recently, the late Hermann Kantorowicz[3] argued that Bracton was a consummate Romanist, using Roman terminology with surprising skill, improving upon its definitions, correcting Justinian, seeing points that Mommsen missed, and systematizing better than his master Azo. Even Mr Richardson (who finds Kantorowicz somewhat extravagant) would yet have us believe that Bracton was at least a junior don in a not very good university.[4]

How can two competent scholars such as Maitland and Kantorowicz draw such opposite conclusions from the same book?

The weak point is in those words 'the same book'. It was not in fact the same book which they were reading. This chapter began with some remarks on the pleasant game of textual criticism, and it must now be disclosed that Kantorowicz was a past-master of that science in all its aspects.[5]

---

[1] *Salomon et Marcolfus*, ed. Walter Benary (Heidelberg, 1914).
[2] Maitland, *Bracton and Azo* (Selden Society, vol. VIII), pp. xviii, xix n. 1.
[3] Kantorowicz, *Bractonian Problems* (Glasgow, 1941).
[4] Cf. his remarks in *English Historical Review*, LIX, 42.
[5] Kantorowicz, *Einführung in die Textkritik* (1921).

There are numerous places where the text of Bracton is beyond all doubt corrupt. The various readings of the different manuscripts are equally unsatisfactory; only conjecture remains. Sometimes an obscurely written word in the original has been variously misunderstood by long successions of copyists. More often (and this is essentially so in a long and laborious task) the copyist works mechanically, heedless of the sense of his text—which indeed he may not comprehend. A scribe familiar with the language of the common law may be baffled by the unfamiliar terminology and abbreviations of the Romanist or canonist. Sometimes a scribe is too ambitious and may introduce 'corrections' into a text which is actually quite accurate—if only he had understood it. More often he is tricked by his eyesight. Thus it is extremely common for the same word (especially in a technical work) to occur twice in close proximity. The scribe will copy a phrase ending with the first occurrence of the word, and at the next glance at his exemplar he will continue copying from the second occurrence of the word, thus omitting the intervening passage. In the sesquipedalian jargon of the textual critics this is familiarly known as homoeoteleuton, which is deemed to be a special case of haplography.

That haplographies abound in the manuscripts of Bracton is not surprising to any one who has dealt with the manuscript transmission of texts; they are very common also in the Year Books and add considerably to the editor's difficulties. In the case of Bracton they can often be restored with confidence when we know for certain that Bracton was copying a particular passage from Azo or the *Institutes*. Otherwise, there may enter a large element of conjecture in emending the text.

If the manuscripts of a work are fairly numerous, there is a good chance that the scribes will not all have haplographized the same passage, and so the lapses of one may be repaired by the diligence of another; and that is generally the case, fortunately, with most ancient and medieval texts.

But, in the case of Bracton, Kantorowicz drew special attention to places where *all* the manuscripts concur in a faulty reading which was itself due to haplography. That is a serious matter, for it shows that the common ancestor of all the manuscripts (the archetype as it is called) was therefore at fault. Now haplography is essentially a trick of the sight; it happens when you copy, not when you compose in the first place. When for the first time

Bracton put his thoughts on to parchment (or perhaps, paper) there may have been all sorts of slips of the pen, but there were no haplographies save where Bracton was at the moment copying from some existing text or treatise; and yet all our extant manuscripts descend from one ancestor which is riddled with them (or so Kantorowicz believed). The conclusion must be that they all derive from one copy which was not Bracton's autograph.

The unknown man who prepared that first copy, with all its errors and haplographies, has been denominated by Kantorowicz as the Redactor, and upon his devoted head are heaped the vices and corruptions of the manuscript text—we remember that the great Bentley himself[1] had postulated over two centuries ago an 'editor' who prepared the blind Milton's *Paradise Lost* for the printer, and incurred the blame for those things which Bentley did not approve in Milton. Kantorowicz calls for a new edition which should eliminate as far as possible, according to the accepted principles of 'transcriptional probability', the errors which the Redactor introduced at the fountain-head of all our manuscripts. He gives us some brilliant examples of the subtle processes by which it can be done. The result is startling. It is no exaggeration to say that Maitland and Kantorowicz were reading two different books: Maitland the bungling, ignorant, careless work of the Redactor which the manuscripts have transmitted to us, while Kantorowicz discerned the luminous, faultless learning of the Master himself. Once the text is restored to its original integrity, Bracton's Romanism is seen to be as good as the best of any age.

Now all that is a fascinating exhibition of textual criticism in which a master displays all his virtuosity. It has provoked an abundant literature—which is all to the good. Moreover, it has posed a genuine problem: we can no longer assess Bracton's class in Roman law until we are sure that we are marking his paper and not the Redactor's.

Was there a Redactor? Woodbine[2] has denied his existence save in the fertile imagination of Kantorowicz. But, after all, Maitland suspected something of the sort some sixty years ago when he was preparing the volume which in 1894 was presented to the Selden Society. He constantly qualifies his remarks as referring to

---

[1] Jebb, *Bentley*, pp. 172 ff.; J. W. Mackail, 'Bentley's Milton', *Proceedings of the British Academy*, XI, 55.

[2] Woodbine, book review, *Yale Law Journal*, LII, 428 ff.

'Bracton, as his text stands';[1] he took his precautions, 'no better version than this has been found of Bracton's text';[2] we must bear in mind the possibility of 'an early copyist of his book' when criticizing what we find there under Bracton's name;[3] we must remember that his manuscript of Azo may sometimes have been to blame;[4] he introduces to his readers his summing-up of the case against Bracton with the words: 'Before an unfavourable judgment is given it will be right for them to remember that they may not yet be reading what Bracton really wrote.'[5] Maitland had long ago made it clear that the text of Bracton presented considerable difficulties which made him cautious in dealing with the question of Bracton's Romanism. The theory of a Redactor would not have come as a surprise to him.

There are places, indeed, where only the hypothesis of the Redactor will account for the present state of the text. That need not mean that one Redactor garbled the whole of Bracton's text; nor need it mean (although that seems to be the general view) that the Redactor necessarily worked after Bracton's death. If the existence of the Redactor is accepted, one is bound to ask why he did not fix the position (be it right or wrong) where the numerous *addiciones*—and indeed, large vagrant sections of text—were to appear in the archetype which he was preparing. If he was working after Bracton's death, and if it was the manuscript which he prepared which was to be the archetype from which all existing manuscripts derive, then one would expect a much greater uniformity among them than in fact they show. This difficulty should be remembered when we consider, in the next chapter, the remarkable treatment of dower and the varying places where that treatment is to be found in different manuscripts.

The Redactor certainly did not succeed in concealing the facts that Bracton did not finish his book, and was himself revising it at various dates, notably by inserting *addiciones* from time to time. Nor did the Redactor fix in their place many of the loose slips and notes which he would have had to deal with if he were engaged upon a definitive version of a dead scholar's papers and were preparing the archetype of all our manuscripts. Bracton led a busy life, con-

---

[1] Maitland, *Bracton and Azo* (Selden Society, vol. VIII), p. 41.
[2] *Ibid.* p. 76.   [3] *Ibid.* p. 77.
[4] *Ibid.* pp. xxxiv, 105; and for Azo's *Lectura*, see F. de Zulueta, in *Studi Bonfante*, III, 268.   [5] *Ibid.* p. xvii.

stantly travelling the length of southern England; he must have had to rely heavily on one or (more probably) several clerks, and had scant opportunity of correcting their work. In that sense, there may have been several 'redactors' at work during his lifetime. Such a hypothesis will explain the traces which are certainly to be found at various places in the book, and will also account for the fact that although errors may be conspicuously fixed in the text, nevertheless many passages, large or small, are vagrant in the surviving manuscripts. The textual situation was certainly very complicated; but until we know much more about the text it is unsafe, and probably unjust, to disparage Bracton's Roman learning.

We still have three-quarters of Bracton's large work on our hands, wherein he discusses in minute detail the English law of actions. Every page attests his complete mastery of an enormous mass of crabbed and technical detail. He may well have 'got up' sufficient Roman law for his purpose by mere diligence and a good text-book, but this formidable mass of detail on English procedure could not be acquired, still less mastered and systematized, without spending a lifetime in its administration. Nor was that enough. There may well have been a dozen men in Bracton's day whose knowledge of procedure was as extensive and as exact as his; but they neither did nor could write such a book. In the first place, they lacked the analytic power to marshal so much detail; for another thing, they had no *Note Book*.

The discovery and identification by Vinogradoff[1] of *Bracton's Note Book*, and the superb editing of it by Maitland, have resulted in a flood of new light being thrown, not only upon the law, but also upon Bracton's approach to the law. Into that book he caused several scribes to copy some two thousand cases from the plea rolls, especially from the rolls of Pateshall and his own master Rayleigh. It sometimes happens that the original rolls survive with his markings on them.[2] Many of the cases in the *Note Book* are cited in the treatise. Bracton did not rely on 'picking up' his law, nor did he trust to his general recollection of its details. He wanted to be sure; above all, he wanted authority.

In his day, Glanvill had found authority in the writs which

---

[1] Vinogradoff's letter in the *Athenaeum* of 19 July 1884 is reprinted in Maitland, *Bracton's Note Book* (1887), I, xvii–xxiii.

[2] The plates in Lady Stenton's *Eyre Rolls* (Selden Society, vol. LIII) show a page of the manuscript of the *Note Book*, and some of the marked plea rolls.

initiate litigation. In turn, Bracton adds a new type of authority—
cases. The reconstruction of Bracton's early career which is
here suggested is enough to explain how he came to have the rolls
of Rayleigh in his possession for a period prolonged enough to
study them in detail; and recent researches[1] have assembled
enough evidence of the somewhat casual custody of plea rolls at
this date to account for his access to yet other rolls.

Bracton's use of cases has been sufficiently canvassed for conclusions to be drawn, at least upon some matters. It is manifest
that he had no notion of the modern system of using cases as a
source of law; nor does he use cases as the data from which he
ascertains the law by a process of induction. This is apparent, if
only from the fact that the cases he uses are not recent, but
relatively old—mostly about a generation old when he was writing.
He uses them, not because he feels bound by them, but because
he feels the need of authority in the intellectual, rather than the
legal, sense. The fact that English law is not 'written' gave him
a good deal of difficulty, simply because a scientific law-book in
his days rested solidly upon code and digest, *decretum* and decretals.
Our original writs did not go far enough—indeed, they only
reached the threshold of legal proceedings, and left one there.
It would have been temerarious in the extreme to have set out his
treatment of actions with no more scientific basis than his mere
word. Glanvill had not been under the necessity of deciding this
point, because all he needed was to show the authoritative text
which conferred jurisdiction to hear a particular case upon particular judges of the king's court.[2] Bracton tackled the much more
recondite matter of process, and in this bewildering jungle he
sought authority in cases. Not any cases, but carefully selected
cases; not the latest cases, but what seemed to him the best cases—
which in fact were mostly as old as he himself. Indeed he broadly
hints that recent decisions are unsatisfactory, and so he goes back
deliberately to the older and better rules.

[1] Sayles, *King's Bench* (Selden Society, vol. LV), I, cxvi ff., cliv ff.; C. A. F
Meekings, 'Martin Pateshull and William Raleigh', *Bulletin of the Institute of
Historical Research*, XXVI, 157 ff. Note also the important introduction by
Mr Meekings to *Curia Regis Rolls*, XI. Cf. *ibid.* vol. XII.

[2] Like Glanvill before him, Bracton gives the text of writs; but he does not
give the text (nor any part of it) of cases. The form of the pleadings which
constituted the 'record' of an English case did not produce quotable extracts
comparable to the decretals which the canonists collected.

What those differences were, it is less easy to ascertain. Lady Stenton has made a brave adventure in this field,[1] but the results seem meagre. Long ago Maitland made the sly suggestion that 'there may have been Proculians and Sabinians' in English law,[2] by which I understand him to mean a sharp division of opinion over indistinguishable differences. However that may be, it seems that Bracton used cases as scientific or intellectual authorities— since authorities he must have, if he is to write a scientific book— rather than as formal authorities binding upon the courts.

One of Bracton's major contributions, therefore, lies in his lengthy treatment of the minute details of practice and procedure. Continental legal studies were taking the same turn. Roman and canon law were developing vastly detailed systems of procedure which were framed upon the elaborate models of Rome and Byzantium. They found them scientifically interesting, and soon succumbed to the temptation of letting pure theory override the practical requirements of contemporary life. If Bracton had wanted to romanize English law he would have started by injecting the work of the procedural experts of his day into his treatment of the law of actions. There is not the slightest trace of that; his authorities are the native writs and plea rolls and nothing else.

This assignment of three-quarters of his space to procedural detail had a further effect. It compelled Bracton to separate substance from procedure and to treat his tripartite scheme as being (for practical purposes) only bipartite. That is to say, his first hundred folios or so are devoted to substantive law. That was momentous. The faculty of seeing law as principles, with procedure strictly subordinate, is a decisive step towards legal maturity. True it is that Glanvill had already achieved this, under the stress of a sharp crisis in legal history, in his remarkable Book VII. But he did it in spite of himself, and his plan made no provision for it. He ought to have been commenting upon writs; but there were no settled writs as yet for the new law of family property, and he had to go beyond, far beyond, the authorities which he professed to follow.

Bracton felt no such difficulty. He speculated (in the medieval sense of the word) not from necessity but from choice. His initial

---

[1] In *Eyre Rolls* (Selden Society, vol. LIII), xxii ff.

[2] Maitland, *Bracton's Note Book*, I, 52. For a list of points on which they differed, see Bonfante, *Histoire de droit romain*, II, pp. 282–8.

plan deliberately separated the law of things from the law of actions and he took that to mean the separation of substantive law from procedural law. The magnitude of that achievement is the measure of Bracton's contribution to English legal science. It might have had grave results. It might have deposed procedure into the position of mere mechanism designed to give effect to legal principles—which indeed is now the proper place of procedure. To have done that prematurely might have caused serious trouble: it would have abandoned the only part of our law which was structurally solid, in favour of principles which had not yet achieved sufficient stability to stand (as they ought to stand) alone. Bracton did not let that tempting vision beguile him. With sure judgment, he gave us our substantive principles, but his cross-references make it clear that, to him, cases illustrated not only procedural but substantive law as well. His book therefore suffers no dichotomy but is a well-knit whole. The first part foreshadows all our text-books; the second part, all our books of practice.

It was too good to last. It is the end of a tradition which runs from *Quadripartitus* and the *Leges Henrici Primi* through Glanvill to Bracton—a tradition rooted in general scientific method as applied by the Middle Ages to all the major fields of study, a tradition in all its essentials academic. Already in Bracton's lifetime a new type of book was appearing. It is the work of men most of whom know nothing at first hand of Roman or canon traditions of scholarship, whose approach is completely unacademic, who are immersed in the details of practice, and try simply to transmit these details to their professional pupils. These little books made a fresh start in our legal writing. They sought out fresh authorities of their own choosing and started a new process which within a few years of Bracton's death was to give us the Year Books.

CHAPTER IV

BRACTONIAN PROBLEMS

In the course of a general survey of Bracton's life, it has been suggested that his legal career was preponderantly that of a common lawyer, and not that of a civilian or a canonist. Then, turning from the man to the book, we examined its structure and method from the point of view which has been applied to the earlier literature throughout this course, namely, its arrangement and the nature of the authority upon which it is based—all this, moreover, to be considered as part of the principal theme which is the origin, the nature, and the influence of the text-book in legal history.

Even so broad a survey as that could not avoid mentioning the fundamental problems which confront every student of Bracton. It seemed no exaggeration to say that Maitland and Kantorowicz reached opposite conclusions about Bracton because they were not reading the same book; Maitland read the manuscripts, but Kantorowicz read what he believed to be the true Bracton concealed beneath the hopeless mass of corruption contained in them.

There are many reasons for pursuing that matter a little further. Primarily of course because it is essential to any use of Bracton at all, for any purpose. But broader considerations are involved. Apart from the interests of a few Bractonian specialists, or even of medievalists in general, there is a much larger issue before us, namely, the whole process by which a book comes into being. The printed page of the Bible, of Virgil, of Shakespeare, of any modern writer is the point at which the general reader begins; but in fact it is the point at which, for the author, a long process of creation ends. To get behind the printed page with its received text is often the only means of ascertaining the true text and the true meaning of a work. The nature and method of the inquiry is basically the same for all texts, ancient or modern, literary or technical, and experience of one investigation may very well help in others.

We can begin with the first problem which readers of Bracton are likely to encounter: the *addiciones*. These are passages written at a later date than the main text, which have become incorporated into the vulgate text and are at first sight indistinguishable from it in the printed page. Often they are the work of a later commentator; sometimes they are genuine afterthoughts of the author himself. In either case, there is the risk that an *addicio* may get inserted in the wrong place. Bracton is not the only author to have suffered from this mishap. It befell Maitland himself when certain of his lectures came to be printed after his death under the title of *Equity*. The passage seems not to have been suspected heretofore. This is how it appears on the printed page:[1]

...we find the famous John of Gaunt disposing by his will of lands which are held to his use by feoffees. We find that Henry of Bolingbroke, afterwards Henry IV, is a *cestui que use* and Gascoigne C.J. is one of his feoffees. He provides for Thomas, John and Joan Beaufort, his illegitimate children, with the remainder over to his right heirs.

Now we may be sure that Maitland neither wrote nor spoke such nonsense. He knew as well as we all know that the Beauforts were not the children of Henry IV but of John of Gaunt. How then did such a blunder come to be printed? The editors who prepared Maitland's *Equity* for the printer were fallible but honest men, and in their preface they explain that they have used the notes of some of Maitland's hearers as well as his own. In putting this material together they confess to having an uneasy feeling that 'in our incorporation of them into his text there must be errors'. This passage is certainly one of them, and it is easy to see how the error came about. The sentence about Henry IV is obviously an *addicio* which has been put into the wrong place in the text. Take it out, and the rest is correct, for 'he' and 'his' then relate naturally to John of Gaunt, as Maitland undoubtedly meant them to. The proper place for the sentence about Henry IV is at the end of the whole passage. This curious little incident serves to show that the transmission of a text may go astray just as much in the twentieth as in the thirteenth century, and that textual criticism may illuminate a modern law-book as well as the Bible or the classics.

In Bracton the *addiciones* are much more numerous, but fortunately easy to trace in most cases. There are about fifty manuscripts of Bracton extant, and they fall roughly into three classes in their

---

[1] See p. 30 of the first edition, 1909, by A. H. Chaytor and W. J. Whittaker; pp. 29–30 of the second edition, 1936, revised by J. W. Brunyate.

treatment of any one *addicio*. There are, first, those which do not contain it. Then there are those which contain the *addicio* in the margin or on a small slip of parchment inserted since the book was made up. Finally there are those which contain the additional matter in the body of the text, sometimes accompanied by a note that it is an *addicio*, and sometimes not. A careful collation of the manuscripts therefore reveals most of those passages which are or once were recognized by early scribes as being additions.[1] It will also be clear that the normal career of an *addicio* is to begin in the margin or on a slip of parchment, and finally to get into the body of the text.

Where did they come from? Many of them are the reflexions or elaborations of readers; but some of them are certainly by Bracton himself. The extraneous additions are sometimes unmistakable. They may expressly refer to the legislation of Edward I. They may begin 'Note...', 'Look...', 'Here you see...', 'What is said here...', or similar words with which one man comments on the work of another.

. Others have beginnings which might equally be the comment of a learned reader or the author's own after-thought: 'Because...', 'But if...', 'Similarly...', and the like. In some seventy instances the *addicio* contains a reference to a case—and one immediately thinks of the tendency of every law-writer to slip in an additional case at the last moment. Bracton sometimes did it, but more often it was a reader who slipped them in, and sometimes the cases are after Bracton's day. Even cases fom the *Note Book* may have been intruded into the treatise by a later hand, for the *Note Book*, like the treatise, began its wanderings from hand to hand as soon as Bracton died.

There is a further factor which has immensely complicated the transmission both of the text and of the *addiciones*. This is due to the immense demand for copies of Bracton's treatise. The simple process (much used for smaller works) of borrowing or hiring a copy and then setting one's clerk to copy it out in his spare moments was much too slow for so long a book. Readers were in a hurry to get it, and would not wait. Much time could be saved by having four, five or six scribes simultaneously at work on different sections of the text; this was possible since already it was possible to

---

[1] Such passages have been listed in Woodbine's edition of Bracton, I, 372. In his text Woodbine distinguishes them by angular brackets.

assemble the four, five or six copies that would be needed (unless there were a single copy unbound). A system like that is a bit difficult to organize, but it was often used; clearly it is suggestive of the commercial stationer in a university town where the demand for copies, and the available supply of exemplars, were both considerable.[1]

The effect of that upon the text is disconcerting. It is no longer possible to say that MS. *P* is derived from MS. *Q*, or indeed to classify the manuscripts into families; any one manuscript may have different pedigrees in different parts of its text. Even if it is transcribed throughout in one hand, it may yet have been derived from an exemplar which was itself produced in the commercial way. The effect is still more confusing upon the *addiciones*. The copy you have just bought may have some in the margin copied from the exemplar; or you may have told the scribe to put them into the text and so make a tidier book. When you use the book you may make additions of your own, or you may copy the additions from a friend's copy. The result is that the additions often do not belong to the same manuscript tradition as the text which they accompany.

The chaotic state of Bracton's text is itself an indication, therefore, of the immense demand for the book as soon as it became available, with the result that commercial as well as the more ordinary methods were applied to its multiplication, and the further result that a pedigree of the manuscripts cannot be constructed.

The fate of Bracton's book in the thirteenth century was not unlike that which befalls a modern successful law-book. Take as an example Stephen's *Commentaries* of which first the author, and then subsequent lawyers, have produced a score of editions. But if it is asked whether Serjeant Stephen wrote a particular phrase, and if not, who did, then there is only one answer: nobody knows and nobody cares. Stephen has long been a name and nothing more; his book pursues its own life into a new age independently. Likewise Bracton. Nobody felt any concern at preserving the ·original text. Everybody wanted as useful a text as possible, and so *addiciones* multiplied.

---

[1] On the vital role of the *stationarii* with their master-copies in the transmission of great medieval texts, see J. Destrez, *La Pecia dans les manuscrits universitaires du XIIIe et du XIVe siècle* (Paris, 1935).

It is universally admitted that some of these additions come from Bracton himself. Yet it is difficult to formulate any precise tests by which to settle the paternity of any particular *addicio*. Maitland hardly attempted it. Woodbine did something, but a great many cases are insoluble, and the sense or feeling of an editor like Woodbine, who spent a lifetime with the text, is as near as one can get to a decision whether this or that addition is from the master's hand. There is one indication of a general character, however, which is sometimes helpful. The *consensus* of a group of manuscripts which have little or none of the additional matter in the text is some indication of the original contents of the text. This group has been isolated by Woodbine as being 'the nucleus of Group I' in his classification.[1]

That group of manuscripts is closely associated with another problem. The manuscripts of that group represent an early state of the text, and it is believed that Bracton himself introduced a number of changes, some of them verbal or stylistic, others involving *addiciones* of some length, after it got into circulation. Later on there were other additions made, perhaps in successive waves. If the principal additions could be assigned to one or another of these waves, and if the waves could be put into chronological order, a great advance would be made in the textual criticism of Bracton. But that seems hardly possible.

Even when there is a general *consensus* of good manuscripts, and no significant variant reading, there may yet be grave difficulty. It has been suggested by Kantorowicz that there are places where the testimony of the manuscripts is unassailable—and yet the text is hopelessly at fault because it says something which is demonstrably wrong, something that Bracton could not have written. If that is indeed the textual situation of Bracton's treatise as a whole, then there seems to be no way of accounting for it, except the theory of the Redactor which Kantorowicz propounded. The essentials of that theory are:

(*a*) all our manuscripts descend from one archetype;
(*b*) that archetype was not Bracton's original;
(*c*) it was prepared by a Redactor after 1268 when Bracton died;
(*d*) the Redactor was more than a scribe, less than a scholar;
(*e*) he was competent in English law but ignorant of Roman law;
(*f*) he worked from Bracton's autograph;

---

[1] Woodbine's edition of Bracton, I, 302 ff.

(g) even when the autograph was correct, the Redactor sometimes misread it and introduced error into the archetype and hence into all its descendants;

(h) much of the Redactor's error was due to haplography.

Of haplography I spoke briefly on a previous occasion. The Redactor was addicted to this vice in an exceptional degree and achieved some astonishing results—comparable in their disconcerting effects to the masterly use of metathesis by Dr Spooner. His efforts, though multitudinous, involve each of them but a few words. As a curiosity I may mention that in my small experience of these matters the grand slam in haplography was made not by the Redactor, but subsequently by the scribe of MS. Bodley 170. He copied from f. 230 the words '*si autem plures fructuarium*' and continued with '(*fructuarium*) *valebit impetratio*' on f. 261. Evidently he had closed his exemplar, and then reopened it when he continued—but at the wrong page. Still, he remembered the word *fructuarium* and by almost incredible ill luck it occurred on both pages. As a result he skipped no less than eighty-four printed pages of Woodbine's edition.[1] Our Redactor is not accused of anything so spectacular as that, although the cumulative effect of his activities has cost Bracton his reputation, we are told.

The personality of the Redactor, so circumstantially described by Kantorowicz, has been accepted by Professor Schulz,[2] and indeed was foreshadowed by Maitland himself over half a century ago, although on evidence which was (at that time) insufficient. On the other hand, the Redactor's existence is denied by Professor Woodbine[3] and Mr H. G. Richardson.[4] There is no avoiding the issue, therefore; any serious student of Bracton must decide whether the book he reads is by the master, or by his bungling thirteenth-century editor.

Let us consider first of all the evidence for the existence of the Redactor as a general proposition. A good many passages are adduced by Kantorowicz, but it is only possible to deal in a

---

[1] Bracton, ff. 230–61 (ed. Woodbine, III, 185–268). This seems not to be mentioned in this connexion by Maitland, Woodbine or Kantorowicz. It will be observed that, to achieve this result, the scribe of Bodley 170 (or alternatively, the exemplar from which he copied) must have read *fructuarium* instead of *feoffati* in the first occurrence, and instead of *firmarium* in the second occurrence.

[2] F. Schulz, 'A new approach to Bracton', *Seminar*, II, 42.

[3] G. E. Woodbine, book review, *Yale Law Journal*, LII, 439.

[4] H. G. Richardson, 'Studies in Bracton', *Traditio*, VI, 61 at 104.

lecture with one or two of them. Thus we may begin with some words which are among the best known in the whole of the law. The first sentence of Justinian's preface to the *Institutes* says that 'the imperial majesty should not only be furnished with arms, but should also be armed with laws: *non solum armis...sed etiam legibus...*'. Nothing could be simpler than that, or more familiar to the most elementary student. Yet when Bracton uses the phrase on f. 107b it appears as 'the king ought not always to be armed with arms, but with laws: *non semper...armis, sed legibus*'.

Beyond all doubt, that is nonsense. *Non semper* can only be a misreading of *non solum*, and as far as we can be sure of anything, we may be sure that Bracton wrote *non solum*. Yet all the manuscripts concur in the wrong reading. There seems no explanation for that unanimity save that they all derive from one ancestor which contained the error. Bracton's autograph (if there were one, which is by no means sure) may have had an abbreviation for *solum* which the Redactor mistook for an abbreviation of *semper*. But the significant thing is that *all* our manuscripts transmit that initial error.

The error is, of course, trivial, but it is none the less illuminating as a sample of the textual problem which lies between us and the intelligent study of Bracton. The matter becomes more serious, and much more difficult to handle, when we have to suspect such mishaps in passages where Bracton's legal and intellectual quality is at stake.

Bracton's competence in Roman law has long been queried by a succession of scholars whose opinions carry weight. Selden was astonished at Bracton's handling of the *Lex regia*;[1] Holt had to alter the printed text before he could incorporate Bracton's passage on bailment into *Coggs* v. *Bernard*;[2] Holmes could find nothing good to say about Bracton's Roman law (or about Roman law generally, for that matter).[3] It was a systematic confrontation of Bracton's treatise and the Roman texts that led Maitland to pronounce him 'uninstructed'.

And yet, all the time, Maitland was uneasy about his conclusion. Time after time he qualified his remarks by saying 'if we can trust the text' or words of similar import.[4] He went to the manuscripts,

---

[1] Selden's *Dissertatio ad Fletam* (ed. Ogg), pp. 25 ff.
[2] 2 Lord Raym. 909.
[3] O. W. Holmes, *Collected Papers*, p. 155; *Common Law*, p. 175.
[4] Cf. pp. 55–6 above.

and their frequent concurrence in passages which were blatantly bad law seemed to corroborate his finding that Bracton was guilty of writing nonsense.

The contention of Kantorowicz is that the manuscripts are wrong, and never so wrong as when they are all wrong together.

In a lecture it is impossible to enter upon details, for it is only with the texts of Bracton, Azo and the *Corpus Juris* under one's eyes that such arguments can be developed. A short but extreme example is on f. 103, which led Maitland to the conclusion that 'Bracton seems to think that the proprietary action for land is an *actio confessoria*'.[1] There are, it is true, two short consecutive sentences, the former of which might give this impression; the latter gives an entirely correct account of the *actio confessoria*. So Bracton did know perfectly well what such an action was. How then can we account for the former sentence which is complete nonsense? In the first place, we observe that the printed texts have no authority whatever for putting the word 'confessoria' in the sentence. No surviving manuscript contains it, and there is nothing to suggest that Bracton wrote it—nor indeed, the Redactor. In the second place, the sentence lacks a verb, and whether with, or without, the offending word, makes neither grammar nor sense, to say nothing of law. One thing is clear: the common ancestor of all our manuscripts was defective at this point and did not contain the word 'confessoria'. There is certainly no evidence here to show that Bracton did not know what an *actio confessoria* was, more especially as the second of these two sentences explains the term clearly and correctly.

Another short example is on folio 7b where all the manuscripts say that 'No one is forbidden access to the sea shore, as long as they keep away from buildings, since the [shores] are not common'.[2] This nonsense is due to the intrusion of a single word 'litora', shores, which certainly crept in from the margin into the text. Without that word the sentence is perfectly correct, for it is the buildings which we are warned are not common. But all the manuscripts have the blunder, which therefore comes from the

---

[1] Maitland, *Bracton and Azo* (Selden Society, vol. VIII), pp. 176 f.; Bracton (ed. Woodbine), II, 294; Kantorowicz, *Bractonian Problems*, 102.

[2] Maitland, *Bracton and Azo* (Selden Society, vol. VIII), pp. 86–7, 93; Kantorowicz, *Bractonian Problems*, pp. 88–9.

archetype. That the archetype accurately presented Bracton's thought is altogether incredible.

In these and many other passages so keenly analysed by Kantorowicz it seems abundantly proved that behind them all lies a single, very faulty archetype.[1] It now remains to consider what conclusions can be drawn about the Redactor of that mischievous volume.

A multitude of teasing questions immediately arise. First, when did the Redactor do his work? At one time Maitland himself got very near postulating such an archetype, and placed its preparation at some date after 1275, on the grounds that the manuscripts give the dates of limitation of sundry writs as they were settled by the statute of Westminster I. That argument is less cogent than it sounds. The forms of writs were extremely familiar to practitioners, readers and copyists of Bracton, and they must almost unconsciously have modernized the forms they were copying; indeed they had every interest to do so deliberately.

The universal opinion at the present moment (excepting only Professor Woodbine and Mr Richardson, who deny that there ever was a Redactor) is that put forward by Dr Kantorowicz that the Redactor did his work as soon as Bracton was dead, and then put the treatise into circulation by allowing copies to be made. This proposition has not so far been debated, but it certainly ought to be.

There seem to me insuperable difficulties in the suggestion that the Redactor worked after Bracton's death, and that he then— only then—produced the archetype of all our manuscripts. We must remember that if there was an archetype at all (and of that I see no possible doubt) it must have been the archetype of the whole work. Further, the archetype was written, and written as we have seen by a man who was copying, and copying badly. We are, therefore, concerned with a literary executor who arranges and prepares for publication the scattered papers of his testator; the result is necessarily a continuous whole. This situation must be distinguished from that where the executor merely gives access to his testator's papers—in that case every scholar who consults them will solve textual difficulties in his own way. The state of

---

[1] It will be remembered that the great Bentley himself ascribed Milton's asperities, incoherences and 'errors' to an anonymous and hypothetical editor; above, p. 55.

the manuscripts precludes that supposition, and we are bound to envisage a Redactor who himself undertook to edit, to prepare a text, and to clear up difficulties. In the purely common law parts of the work he did so with fair competence; in the Roman law parts he stumbled continually and made a hopeless mess of it. He was not interested, and was not skilled, in that side of the master's work.

Now let us suppose for a moment that the Redactor did work at the date which Kantorowicz assigns to him—the death of Bracton. It immediately follows that the text—the whole text—was settled. The loose papers, the author's after-thoughts and marginal additions, will have been dealt with somehow. They will be in a place fixed for them by the editor of the archetype. It is essential to remember that much of the Redactor's work was done on the main body of the treatise and that that work took the form of copying. In doing that, the Redactor would immediately be confronted with the *addiciones*. There is textual evidence that the Redactor left his mark on them too (or at least on some of those which evidently came from Bracton's hand originally).[1] There could only be one consequence of such an operation: the *addiciones* would be fixed in some certain place. It might be the right place or the wrong one, but fixed they would have to be, and subsequent copies would necessarily put them in the place where the Redactor had left them.

There is one *addicio* so enormous that no one so far seems to have ventured to include it among the hundreds of lesser passages. This is the lengthy treatment of dower, which takes up ff. 296–317b of the vulgate text and occupies fifty-six pages of Woodbine's edition. One of the earliest and best of the manuscripts, Digby 222, does not give it at all. It is also absent from two other manuscripts. Three other manuscripts put the treatise on dower after f. 98 towards the end of the romanesque material. Two more put it at f. 436. Another puts it after f. 438, and yet another puts it at the very end of the whole work. It would seem as though the highly important subject of dower was the last which Bracton wrote—it is certainly a splendid piece of exposition, Bracton at his best. But what was the Redactor doing? If he made the

---

[1] Consequently, if an *addicio* bears traces of the Redactor's work, there is a strong presumption that it is of Bractonian origin, and not the product of some subsequent reader.

archetype which was the parent of all our manuscripts, and prepared it from Bracton's papers after his death, he must have done something with the long section on dower, he must have put this section somewhere, so that it would have a fixed place in the archetype. Yet the omissions of some manuscripts, and the vagaries of others, show clearly that he had done nothing whatever to fix the position of the section upon dower. I cannot escape the conclusion that if the Redactor worked after the death of Bracton, the manuscripts would show much more uniformity than they do.

The textual evidence therefore leaves us in a peculiar position: there must have been a Redactor of an archetype, for his errors and nonsense are to be seen in every extant manuscript. And yet it is impossible to believe that he worked after his master's death, or that he left the work as a whole, in a certain order, which later manuscripts would necessarily have copied from the archetype and from one another.

The answer seems to be that there was a Redactor, but that he was at work during Bracton's lifetime, and not after his death. If during Bracton's lifetime, then necessarily with his knowledge and consent, in constant touch with the author and with the author's papers under his hand, present and taking part in the work of creation. In short, the Redactor is Bracton's clerk or secretary. Let us look at such a man. He has a post of responsibility, and serves a very busy master. Much has been written lately about the immense exertions of the medieval judge. Now Bracton was the most hardworked sort of judge—he did not sit in the comparative quiet of the court of common pleas at Westminster, but spent his official career constantly on the move, either taking assizes in the country, or following the wanderings of the king's own court. An exhausting life, indeed; and on top of it all, he chose to write an enormous book. He drags about with him, backwards and forwards across southern and western England, a small train. For his judicial work he certainly needed clerical assistance— energetic and ambitious young men, no doubt, such as he himself had been in his youth. Upon them he must have drawn for help in compiling his vast volume. We can plausibly imagine the sort of men they were, with their eyes upon a career in law and public affairs, eager and competent, but by no means of an academic turn, passably familiar with the practical side of English law, and cheerfully unaware of the problems of jurisprudence and comparative law.

One of these men Bracton used in writing his book. We can hardly imagine the justice sitting at a table month after month patiently producing the autograph of his book. It is doubtful whether he ever had a period of uninterrupted leisure for any length of time, and to my mind it is very doubtful whether there ever existed an autograph. That Bracton pondered much, we may be sure; that he read extensively in foreign books as well as in bulky plea rolls and in his *Note Book*, is obvious. That his book slowly took shape in his mind long before a word of it was written, is extremely probable. Yet, necessarily, a book is not written all at once. In Bracton's case, the process of composition must have been very intermittent and constantly interrupted by official duties. The ultimate arrangement was to the last unsettled, as his preface explains. Like so many scholars, he hoped for the day when he would have time to put it all into order, revise it, polish it and make a real book of it. But in the meantime his task was to get the stuff down, as and when he could; the rest could wait. How did he work? Almost certainly I think in fits and starts, a few scribbled notes, and then dictation. What the clerk got down on to parchment was as near an autograph as ever existed, I think. In all essentials it was merely the roughest preliminary draft. The writing may well have been shocking: the Elizabethan technical term for it would have been 'foul papers'. Of course, a little later came the stage of 'fair copy' based upon the 'foul papers'. That was the archetype, and that I think is how the Redactor made it.

In saying 'fair copy' I do not mean that it was in any sense ready for press (as one would say nowadays). We can call it 'fair' only in the sense that it was a copy and replaced papers which were 'foul'.[1] In all essentials it was merely a working draft and very far from final. Its interim nature is clear since the author himself continued to make *addiciones* to it. Nevertheless, favoured persons were already given access to it (or contrived to get copies of it) although the book was far from finished; thus a text got into circulation even before the chapter on dower was written. It is beyond all doubt that although Bracton continued to make *addiciones* from time to time, he never revised the work, line by line and word by word. He was a busy man, pressed for time,

---

[1] As a correspondent wrote to Henslowe in 1613: 'I send you the foul sheet and the fair': A. W. Pollard, *Shakespeare's Fight with the Pirates and the Problems of the Transmission of his Text*, p. 56.

and his instinct was to write more and more on subjects yet untouched, rather than to proof-read what he had already written. He may well have overestimated the erudition of his clerk. For straightforward common law, that clerk was perfectly competent, and even if Bracton suspected his proficiency in following a discussion in Romanist language, he might well have decided to let it wait until he himself could go over the whole work thoroughly, as he would have to do, in order to deal with the mounting list of *addiciones*, and indeed to settle the final order of subjects. That, alas, he was never able to do, and so it was only the Redactor's working drafts which became the archetype of all the surviving manuscripts, with all the resulting complications which have worried editors from the sixteenth century until today.

The absence of the chapter on dower from one early manuscript and its varying position in others seems a clear indication that it was one of the last to be written. There is further evidence of this in the chapter itself. On f. 300 b Bracton observes that in very rare cases an action of dower may be postponed to wait the coming of age of the tenant 'as above in the chapter on Exceptions'. From this it would appear, first that 'Dower' was written after 'Exceptions', and secondly that Bracton at one moment contemplated the two chapters appearing with 'Dower' after 'Exceptions'. All the printed editions, and nearly all the manuscripts have nevertheless put 'Dower' earlier (which seems to have been Bracton's first thought; f. 160), so that his indication of *supra* has been falsified.

On a previous occasion I made a suggestion about the first hundred or so folios of Bracton's book. It is, as all the world knows, the portion in which Bracton drew most heavily upon his Roman erudition. I then suggested that this was not vanity, but a serious attempt to separate substantive law from procedure. A statement of principles necessarily involves the preliminary work of analysis, and analysis can only be carried out with the aid of a technical equipment of concepts, and words to express them. Our English legal system was extremely centralized, and at an early date; a large mass of business flowed through the royal courts which had to be dealt with in the heat of the moment, as it arose. Consequently practice had far outstripped theory, and lawyers had had no time to think in broad terms or to systematize the vast mass of detailed procedure which constituted their daily round.

It is not yet possible to guess how Bracton began his work; he may very well have had some sort of idea in his mind from the outset. Certainly that idea became much more clear to him as the work proceeded, and, in the chapter on dower (where I think we see some of his latest and maturest work), it is expressed in deliberate and measured language in the opening words which have already been set forth.[1] In those words Bracton makes a clear distinction between the substantive law of dower and the procedural details of the action. Moreover, that distinction is not only in his mind, but is structurally expressed in his book, for he has indeed already treated the substantial matters mentioned at considerable length on ff. 92–8.

Now it is to be observed that the long passage 'On the acquisition of property', like that on dower itself, is a vagrant among the manuscripts. A number of them put the whole, or a large part of it after the section on dower, or later still in the work. It is certainly suggestive that the only two considerable portions which are vagrant in their position in the manuscripts are 'Dower' and 'Acquisition of Property', and that it is just those two portions which show the highest degree of integration, with the substantive law fully developed in the one, leaving purely procedural matter for the other.[2] Here at least (and, I think, at last) Bracton succeeded in his aim of writing an ideal text-book, governed by the analysis of principles and their statement in general terms. The task was novel as far as English law was concerned, and although he saw in general what ought to be done, he did not immediately discover how to do it.

Thus his earlier treatment of possession was strictly subordinate to his major theme of donations, which led him to *traditio* (and it is here that he deals with possession), thence to incorporeal things, and thence back to the main subject with more matter on donations. Consequently, when he came to write about the assize of novel disseisin he found that the general principles were not adequately covered, and so here (and also in his treatment of mort dancestor) he had to embark upon a further exploration of principle. When he came to dower, it worked out much better, possibly because he

[1] Above, p. 51.
[2] The words with which Bracton introduces the writ of right at the foot of f. 328 look back to the petty assizes and to the writs of entry, but make no mention of dower. Can it be that he left the writ of right half-finished in order to turn to his novel treatment of the acquisition of property, and dower?

had gained more experience, and also because, in his treatment of the acquisition of property, dower was the last topic dealt with. As is well known, it is in that portion (the first hundred or so folios) where the textual problems abound. It is highly probable that it was constantly being revised from the point of view of distributing matter between the two headings of things and actions.

The great enterprise was unfinished. He did the intensely original and fruitful section on acquisition of property, the like of which had never been seen before in English legal literature, a real *Institutes*. He did the petty assizes, dower and entry and then tackled the enormous subject of the writ of right, its summonses, its essoins, its defaults, its vouchers, its exceptions. Whether these hundred and eleven folios have exhausted Bracton's learning on the writ of right, it is difficult to say. The last five folios seem to introduce the personal actions, but of debt, trespass and so on Bracton gives us no systematic treatment.

From what has already been said, it will be clear that one cannot usefully discuss the 'date' of Bracton unless some necessary qualifications are made. The making of a book so large and so carefully thought upon, by an author so occupied in public labours and so constantly engaged in travel, is obviously the work of many years, some parts of which must be older, others more recent. Add to this the fact that Bracton was involved in church as well as in state, and allow for the turbulence of foreign and domestic politics, and it will be seen that the composition of the book must have been the work of a devoted and determined author who had to make the very most of his scanty leisure. Further, it must not be thought that this (or, indeed, many other books) would be the result of systematic composition beginning with folio 1 and ending with folio 444; a book may often be written in a different order from that in which it finally appears; the preface, especially, is likely to be the most recent, although its position may suggest that it is the earliest part of the work.

In the case of Bracton we naturally look for those periods when he could most probably have snatched time to write—and soon the nature of his early career becomes important: was he an ecclesiastic studying Roman or canon law at Oxford? Or did he spend his youth in the clerical administration of the common law? Some light has been sought upon these problems by noting the books which Bracton used. Kantorowicz[1] fastened upon the connexion with William of Drogheda—a law don at Oxford who was murdered by a servant in 1245—and suggests that Drogheda's preface is derived in part from Bracton's. It must therefore be earlier than Drogheda's death in 1245 and, indeed, earlier still (for other reasons): 1239 is the date Kantorowicz propounds, saying that the treatise 'was written before 1239 by Bracton the clerk of William Raleigh'. This dating puts the work in Bracton's early years of common-law apprenticeship, and differs from Maitland's much later date of 1256.

Mr Richardson[2] would place the borrowing the other way: he would suggest that Bracton on the contrary borrowed from Drogheda whom he would have met at Oxford, and subsequently used a copy with a late additional 'epistle'. On both sides there is much speculation; the essential point to remember seems to be that one can rarely 'date' a book which has slowly matured and been constantly under the author's hand for many years, and that different parts of it may come from different years. Maitland let us see that sort of consideration in the back of his mind when he wrote the cautious but masterly pages on the date of the treatise in *Bracton's Note Book*; his conclusion was that Bracton was seriously engaged on his work after 1250, was making alterations as late as 1254, but ceased to revise it as a whole after 1256.[3]

In pondering this question of date, we must beware of too easily making assumptions—of assuming that the *Note Book* must have been finished before the treatise was begun, that the preface was the first to be written, and that in some unexplained way the treatise had a 'date' which we could attach to it (if only we knew what that date was). It would also be prudent to observe carefully the language which Maitland and Kantorowicz used. The one is concerned to show us that Bracton was 'at work' at one date and 'revised' or 'ceased to revise' certain passages at other dates; the other is concerned to show that 'Bracton must have begun to write his treatise before 1239'. The deduction from the Drogheda connexion is not convincing; nevertheless, it may well be that Bracton was already thinking—perhaps even writing—about

---

[1] Kantorowicz, *Bractonian Problems*, pp. 27–33 (assuming that Drogheda began with the preface when he began to write in 1239).

[2] H. G. Richardson, 'Azo, Drogheda and Bracton', *English Historical Review*, LIX, 22–47.

[3] Maitland, *Bracton's Note Book*, I, 33–44.

English law in 1239, and was revising and amending it as late as 1256 although to the very end he had to leave it unfinished.

Enormous and costly as it was, scores of copies of Bracton were made during the next two generations. They were deeply studied, annotated, commented upon; one is furnished with a lavish gloss by John de Longueville shortly after the year 1300, in a manuscript in Cambridge, Dd. vii. 6. At least one other work, a short tract on consanguinity by Johannes de Deo, has been incorporated in Bracton's text by some manuscripts;[1] on the other hand several portions of Bracton have become detached and pursue a separate existence, a fate which befell Glanvill and *Brevia Placitata*. Many manuscripts show the attempts of owners to bring their Bracton up to date by embodying the results of the radical statutes of Edward I; many others combine this aim with that of shortening the work into more manageable proportions. Some of these efforts achieved so much success that they became independent works with sufficient new and original matter added to justify their pretensions. Frequently the name of an eminent Edwardian judge has become associated with them with the implication that he was the author.

The two tracts known as Hengham *Magna* and Hengham *Parva* are examples.[2] The *Magna*, in spite of its name, is a slight affair of barely fifty pages, intensely practical, and confined to the procedure on a writ of right. The *Parva*, a mere twenty pages, looks like a continuation on a still more modest scale dealing briefly with matters not comprised in the *Magna*—essoins, dower, petty assizes, escheat, entails, and some miscellanea. There is no legal theory in Bracton's grand manner, and not enough detail for a practitioner's book; we can only conclude that it was a student's book, and a very popular one, for some seventy manuscripts are known. The date of the *Magna* may be before 1267, the *Parva* between 1285 and 1290.

Immensely popular as Hengham *Magna* was, there were some who saw the need for something intermediate in size between the full-size Bracton and Hengham's diminutive nutshell. Several serious and well-thought-out attempts were made with the double

---

[1] See Maitland's unsigned note in *Law Quarterly Review*, II, 278 (and cf. *Bracton's Note Book*, I, 27 n. 5).

[2] Both were first edited with still useful notes by Selden in 1616 and are appended to his edition of Fortescue's *De laudibus*; the modern edition (the first which is not attached to the *De laudibus*) is *Radulphi de Hengham Summae*, ed. W. H. Dunham (Cambridge, 1932).

object of reducing the bulk of Bracton and of including the changes and new material consequent upon the legislation of Edward I. The first of these goes by the name of *Fleta*.[1] The first of his many merits is that he was not frightened by Bracton's theoretical discussions; another is the care and thoroughness with which he incorporated the legislation of Edward I; the greatest is in certain entirely original contributions. One of these is a long description of the law-courts and the royal household evidently written from intimate first-hand knowledge. Another is a systematic treatment of the routine of estate management familiar to economic historians as a detached work (in French, instead of in Latin) under the name of Walter of Henley. *Fleta* is now receiving some of the attention which he has long deserved. A new edition for the Selden Society is being prepared by Mr Richardson and Professor Sayles, which will supersede the perfunctory and careless text published in the seventeenth century under Selden's name. These two editors, when they come to write their introduction, will doubtless consider the question whether the section on husbandry is original to *Fleta*, or (as has been supposed hitherto) the interpolation into *Fleta* of a Latin version of a pre-existing treatise by the so-called Walter of Henley.[2] The identity of the author hiding behind the name of *Fleta* has long intrigued historians: Mr Denholm-Young has made out a persuasive case for Matthew of the Exchequer.[3] The fact that only one manuscript of *Fleta* has come down to us suggests that its merits (possibly its language) failed to win it a public.

That last sentence is equally true of another venture of about the same date by a much more eminent author, Gilbert of Thornton, chief justice of the King's Bench in 1290. We first hear of his *Summa* when Selden described a much mutilated manuscript of it in 1647.[4] Nothing more is heard until 1909 when Woodbine suggested that an abbreviated text of Bracton in the library of Lincoln's Inn might be by Thornton (although it does not say so).[5]

---

[1] The first edition is by Selden (1647). A new edition with a translation by H. G. Richardson and G. O. Sayles has begun to appear in the Selden Society's series.

[2] The latest published views on the matter are to be found in D. Oschinsky, 'Medieval treatises on estate management', *Economic History Review*, VIII, 307.

[3] N. Denholm-Young, 'Who wrote "Fleta"?', *English Historical Review*, LVIII, 1; LIX, 252 reprinted in his *Collected Papers*, pp. 68 ff.

[4] Selden, *Dissertatio ad Fletam* (ed. Ogg), pp. 9, 15–17.

[5] Woodbine, 'The *Summa* of Gilbert of Thornton', *Law Quarterly Review*, XXV, 44.

That manuscript certainly belonged to the Thornton family, however. Thornton's *Summa* finally turned up, in private hands, and is now in the Harvard Law Library.[1] Of it I need say no more, for it is being edited for the Ames Foundation by Professor Thorne.[2]

Very different is the book called 'Britton'.[3] Alone of all the epitomes of Bracton, it is in French instead of Latin. That must have been one important factor in the immense success of the book. The change reflects a social change which, after hanging in the balance for a generation, had finally been brought to a decision. The clerical lawyer with his fluent Latin and contacts with canonist and civilian learning, who served the king, indeed, but took his rewards in ecclesiastical preferment, gave way to a newer type of lay lawyer, with some but not very much Latin, who was more at home in French. In other words, there arose a generation which lacked Bracton's background, and wanted its law in the vernacular. The success of Britton and the failure of *Fleta* and Thornton seem best explained by such considerations as these, for otherwise the three works pursue the same policy, and all lean heavily on Bracton.

Britton seems the most neatly arranged of the three, and is a model of clarity and conciseness. The extraordinary fancy of putting the whole work in the king's mouth as a code—complete with writ ordering its observance—is not an afterthought by a later hand (as it was with the *Établissements de St Louis*), but apparently an original feature from the beginning. That such a book with such a pretension should have appeared in the reign of Edward I without protest has never been explained. Nor has its claim ever been taken seriously.

But Britton is the end of an age. The massive, learned, cosmopolitan Bracton was the product of a more spacious epoch. Even abridged and cleverly vulgarized, his book soon ceased to be the principal intellectual fare of English lawyers. The revolution in legal literature was in the fulness of time to produce our most original contribution to legal science, the Year Books. But in between came a group of tracts which is only just coming to be studied; the consideration of these little works must be our next concern.

[1] Plucknett, 'The Harvard manuscript of Thornton's *Summa*', *Harvard Law Review*, LI, 1038.

[2] S. E. Thorne, 'Gilbert de Thornton's *Summa de Legibus*', *University of Toronto Law Journal*, VII, 1.

[3] First printed in 1534. Ed. F. M. Nichols (1865).

CHAPTER V

FRESH BEGINNINGS

THE last chapter brought us to the end of a story, but before embarking upon the sequel a backward glance will be useful as a reminder both of the results achieved, and of the ground lost by the time of Edward I's accession.

The theme has been the beginnings of English legal science, that is to say, of the effort to write of our law in an orderly manner, relating its different parts systematically, and of separating the substance from the multitude of procedural details. From the primitive stage of the Anglo-Saxon period there was a slight progression to the *Leges Henrici Primi*, whose author did indeed recognize the Anglo-Saxon texts as *authoritates*, and added to them some other documents as well; but having done so he was at a loss to marshal his material. With Glanvill we enter the new post-Conquest world. Whoever wrote that book, he had no doubt that his authorities were the common-law writs, and he framed his book upon them, with a careful and sensible distinction between those which initiate proceedings in the king's court, and those which merely transfer to it proceedings begun elsewhere. Order and clarity are his characteristics, and in one place, at least, he shows conspicuous originality in venturing upon substantive law when his writs fail him.

Bracton took immense strides in the direction of scientific exposition. Where Glanvill had confined himself to what would now be called the law of actions, Bracton devoted a quarter of his book to the law of things, and in that quarter he made valiant efforts to state our law in general terms, as a body of principles, independently of the actions which served to enforce them. There he frankly followed the best continental models, but his authorities are still the common-law writs. True he had collected many cases and used them, but not as if they had been decretals and therefore authorities. To Bracton, cases were useful illustrations but not in themselves sources of law. Bearing this in mind, it thus becomes all the more remarkable that he should have generalized so extensively, considering the paucity of strictly authoritative texts.

Finally, I have suggested that Bracton is Latin, Roman and clerical in tradition—the last great example in English law. Like most medieval law-books, it was epitomized, and in part translated. In Normandy, the nearly contemporary *Summa de Legibus* was also translated from the original Latin into the vernacular; indeed, it was further transformed into verse—but that indignity Bracton escaped.

The growing preference for French over Latin is seen in many quarters. Even Glanvill was finally put into French, and brought up to date. The statutes, at first in Latin, became generally French towards the end of Edward II's reign, and if the old departments clung to Latin records, the newer ones turned to French. The only portion of *Fleta* which reached the medieval public was his treatment of agriculture, which circulated—in French instead of the original Latin—under the name of Walter of Henley. All this seems to betoken a radical change in the social habits of those who used English legal material. For one thing it suggests that law and business are sharing the services of a new class of lettered laymen who understand Latin but are really fluent only in French. We need not expect to find, all at once, a profession of legal specialists whose work is entirely and strictly legal. That was indeed to come, but for a long time (and especially in the humbler ranks) law was only part of the activities of the universal handy-man or 'clerk'. Administration and office work generally was his field. While men of this type were in minor orders it was natural that they should be equally active in the local courts of both church and state. An interesting illustration is to be seen in a little treatise recently published in the sixtieth volume of the Selden Society.[1]

One natural line along which such mixed practices might have divided into separate specialisms would have been for all the legal work to go one way, leaving the miscellaneous business and secretarial work to go the other. If that had happened, it would have meant that church and lay courts would have continued to be served by the same men, equally familiar with both. Some mutual influences between the two legal systems would be inevitable, as can be seen from the local law of many places where this situation prevailed. In fact, the line of division in England was generally drawn, not between law and administration, but

---

[1] 'Consuetudines Diversarum Curiarum', in H. G. Richardson and G. O. Sayles, *Procedure without Writ* (Selden Society, vol. LX), pp. cxcv ff.

between the ecclesiastical administrator–lawyer and the secular administrator–lawyer.[1] The rapid development of ecclesiastical law under academic influences widened the breach. The cosmopolitan outlook of Bracton therefore became less possible for the purely English laywer, and all the more so because this division was taking place at the top as well as in the lower reaches of the legal world. The traditional 'king's clerk' was finding more and more laymen among his colleagues and among those laymen were some who were promoted to the bench of the king's courts. It was thus possible to rise to lucrative and dignified places in the king's legal and administrative service alone, without seeking the additional qualifications which the church was finding it easier to exact, now that the universities had large and flourishing schools of canon and civil law.

It was this development which made English law insular, and for so long cut us off from the main stream of Continental juristic science. Of that grave change the change in language from Latin to French is merely an outward indication. It is, of course, impossible to assign precise dates to such events as these. We can say that at the death of Henry III the bench was almost wholly clerical, and that at the death of Edward I it was half lay, and rapidly ·becoming wholly so. The serjeants who had the important business under Edward I were likewise becoming lay, and that implies that for a generation there had been in training a body of lay lawyers. If we take language as the test, then we have already the beginning of French treatises on law soon after 1260, while in the 1270's we get reports of cases in French, and the French translation of Glanvill dates from 1265. The revolution had therefore begun in the last years of Bracton's own lifetime.

The investigation of the non-Bractonian literature of the later thirteenth century is a difficult but fascinating task. Some examples are already in print, although edited only summarily. Many lie in the great libraries in manuscript, and are not easily catalogued or identified.

Fortunately one of the earliest, and certainly one of the most significant examples of this type of legal literature has recently been

---

[1] As it has been remarked recently, 'The appointment of lay stewards and bailiffs was in answer to injunctions given by Archbishop Peckham who aimed at preventing the monks from living outside the monasteries': Dorothea Oschinsky, 'Medieval treatises on estate management', *Economic History Review*, VIII, 304.

edited with great care under the title of *Brevia Placitata*, by the late G. J. Turner, who was engaged upon it (with lengthy intermissions) for half a century.[1] The first thing we notice is that it goes under a variety of titles; some manuscripts call it *Breves Pleidez*, or *Pleez en Franceys*, or *Brefs Enromancees*. The more convenient Latin title under which it is generally known seems to be the invention of Maitland. Further, it exists in a number of successive rescensions as one lawyer after another undertook to enlarge it. Some of these versions are inflated by the inclusion of portions of other works. It is characteristic of our older lawyers that when they found a book useful, they took it in hand and added to it anything else which seemed likely to increase its value. The ruthless scale on which this was done to *Brevia Placitata* is good evidence of its wide use and real value to thirteenth-century lawyers.

There are several indications that the tract was first composed in or shortly after the year 1260. There are some intriguing proper names in the early versions. There is John fitz Geoffrey who may be the son of the still more famous Geoffrey fitz Peter;[2] now John for some years was justiciar of Ireland. To make things more interesting, the model case about an advowson (heard in the common pleas at Westminster) deals with Kilkenny. Other indications point to Lynn in Norfolk, to Yorkshire (and John fitz Geoffrey had been sheriff of that county), and to the diocese of Hereford whose bishop (1269–75) was John le Breton and, according to Turner, author of the tract called *Britton*—an old ascription which Nichols rejected many years ago. Teasing as these references are, they seem too obscure and divergent to permit any plausible conclusion as to the authorship of *Brevia Placitata*, in spite of the very clever sleuthing of Mr Turner.

Turning to the tract itself, we observe that the early types run to thirty or sometimes forty pages of print, and that the text is entirely in French. This is notable since there was a feeling in those days that one should not mix languages. Now writs are in Latin and the oral pleadings are in French; but what is to be done if you want to write about both writs and pleadings? One author, as we shall see, felt bound to write two separate tracts—one in

---

[1] *Brevia Placitata*, ed. G. J. Turner (Selden Society, vol. LXVI), 1951.
[2] For the suggestion that Geoffrey fitz Peter was the author of 'Glanvill', see above, p. 30, n. 3.

Latin about the writs, and another in French about the pleadings. *Brevia Placitata* was faced with this problem in an acute form, and adopted a radical solution: the whole work, writs, pleadings and all, had to be in French.[1]

The substance of *Brevia Placitata* is clear and consistent. It consists of writs (translated into French), each writ being followed by the corresponding *encoupement*. That word was on the point of going out of fashion, and was soon replaced by *conte* (count or declaration). This was the formal and very technical statement by the demandant of the nature of his claim. It was generally fuller than the writ, but must in no wise contradict the writ. A fault in the count, or a variance between the count and the writ, was fatal; consequently counts (although delivered orally) had to be drafted with great care. *Brevia Placitata* clings tightly to its professed programme: it is, as its title proclaims, 'writs pleaded'. In most cases it goes one stage further and gives not only writ and count but also the defence (or 'plea' as the later books call it).

For the most part, that is all *Brevia Placitata* gives. It was not in its early form a treatise of any sort, for it gave no expository matter, and the author did not venture to address the reader or express his opinions; it was a formula book pure and simple, a collection of authorities presented without comment. The breadth and depth of Bracton's thought about law is utterly rejected by this unknown writer who took up his pen at the moment when Bracton abandoned his. If Bracton was Latin, Roman and clerical, this author was French, insular and lay. Where Bracton strove to emulate the contemporary Italian masters, this man gave us the primitive, indeed, the archaic, in legal literature. I have entitled this lecture 'Fresh Beginnings' and in truth *Brevia Placitata* takes us back to the antique when it gives us forms, and nothing but forms.

Even so, the author is not entirely invisible. He took a bold decision when he translated the writs into French. He had a Latin Register of Writs in front of him, and every writ in the country was and always had been in Latin. With stubborn determination he 'romanced' them. It must have needed a strong motive for

---

[1] Documents concerning ecclesiastical pleas being edited for the Selden Society by Professor Norma Adams show that proceedings, even in church courts, in the thirteenth century might take place in French for the convenience of the laity of the upper classes.

that, and the motive is not far to seek: the book is addressed to an audience which is at home in French, but not fluent in Latin. It was for the clerks to draft writs and enrol pleadings in Latin; the rising professional lawyers abandoned those tasks to their clerical brethren, and devoted themselves to the vernacular pleading in court. There were already hints that this was going to be an exciting game calling for great skill and offering rich rewards. If *Brevia Placitata* was the first work expressly written for such men, or for men who aspired to a career of that sort, then we need not be surprised at its vernacular language, its total innocence of any sort of erudition, and its concentration on what the practical man wants—reliable forms. There the author did use his skill, for it needed a lawyer of some judgment and experience to decide what forms were reliable.[1]

Beyond that he refused to go. Not only did he eschew any sort of comment, but he refused to contemplate any sort of methodical arrangement. Nor did copyists feel bound to preserve the arrangement of the primitive state. Consequently, no two manuscripts of *Brevia Placitata* present the work in the same order. As in the Registers of Writs themselves, there was no logical or systematic arrangement, and it was some time later than this tract that the Registers settled down to a rough traditional order of matters. Once again, we can only describe as archaic the supreme indifference of this author to the whole question of systematization—of legal science.

The statement that the author offers forms but no comment is very nearly true, but not quite. Upon the writ of right (the first to be treated) there is a fair amount of explanatory matter on the peculiar procedure of that action. A few lines of this were found to be so useful that soon they came to be detached and circulated separately; in the fulness of time they acquired the repute of being a statute, and duly appear in the *Statutes of the Realm*, I, 218 as the *Statutum de Magnis Assisis*.

In the Selden Society edition of *Brevia Placitata* the forms are printed in large type and the comments in smaller type. Merely turning the pages is sufficient to show that the early versions contain extremely little comment; indeed, it seems likely that if the earliest form could be found, it would show the author's evident

---

[1] This is subject to at least one qualification: he made a mess of the action of dower *unde nihil habet*.

intention to have no comment at all. In any case, it is abundantly clear that the later versions show a large intrusion of explanatory and illustrative material. Within a generation of its first appearance, *Brevia Placitata* might assume the form shown in the Harvard text, which contains a large proportion of extraneous matter (some of it drawn from other law tracts) woven into the fabric of *Brevia Placitata*. Such drastic editing by medieval scholars is not unusual, and bears witness to the opinion that the core of the work was sound and profitable, and well worth the labour of revision.

A short example of how *Brevia Placitata* presents its material will also serve to illustrate my next point.[1] Here it is:

This is the writ of aiel.
The king &c. Command *B* that rightly and without delay he render to *A* a messuage and a carucate of land with the appurtenances in *N*, whereof *E*, grandfather of *A* who is his heir, was vested and seised in his demesne as of fee the day that he died. And if *B* does not do this &c.

Encoupement.
This showeth to you *A* who is here, that *B* who is there, wrongly deforces him of a messuage and a carucate of land with the appurtenances in *N*; and wrongly for this, that his grandfather *E* by name was vested and seised thereof in his demesne as of fee, in time of peace, taking the esplees as in corn &c amounting to half a mark and more, as of fee. From *E* the fee descended to *W* as son and heir; from *W* the fee descended to *A* as son and heir, who is now demandant. And if *B* will deny it &c.

Defence.
Tort and force &c., and will defend where and when he ought. And he thinks he is not bound to answer either him or his writ, by reason that *E* empleaded him *B* by writ of right, and that same *E* made a quitclaim and a fine made in the king's court at Westminster before such and such justices, and that same *E* quitclaimed that land to *B* and to all his heirs. And that this is true he is ready &c.

That is evidently pure form, and form of a simple kind. As Turner has remarked, *Brevia Placitata* in its earliest rescension excludes really difficult matters, such as the more complicated sorts of writs of entry. The declarations or counts likewise avoid most of the subtle difficulties which arise when husband and wife or parceners are demandants or tenants. The defences also are of

---

[1] Translated from *Brevia Placitata*, pp. 35–6. (New initials have been used, since those used by the manuscripts are frequently confusing.)

the simplest and commonest kind. Such material naturally will be presented in an impersonal way, as the blankest of blank forms.

Occasionally, as we have already said, the form is not entirely blank: it may contain names, some of them names of real men known to the general historian. We cannot be sure that this means that those historic personages were parties to the proceedings in which their names are inserted—they may be no more than a reminiscence of a public man, of a neighbour, a patron or the like. In moments of bewilderment we may wonder whether they are not false clues cunningly laid to mislead us in the search for author, date and provenance.

Not only do we find names in some of these forms; there are places (even in the earliest known rescension) where we find a scrap of dialogue like this:[1]

> And then said the justice—
> Lady, have you anything else to say?
> No, Sir; I put myself entirely upon your award.
> Lady, wage your law.
> With pleasure, Sir.
> Find pledges.

That is still, in a sense, common form, for that sort of conversation, if briefly reported, could hardly take any other shape. But the aspect changes when we find (still in the earliest rescension) that 'La Justice' is Sir Roger of Thurkelby (who died in 1259) in one case, and Gilbert of Preston in another. By the time we get to the second rescension the trend is unmistakable: we find more names (notably the Prior of Kilkenny v. the Abbot of Mordon), and when we get to the later rescensions the blank forms are often replaced by reports of genuine cases. The Harvard text with which the volume concludes has several choice and genuine cases.[2] In short, the collection of a formula book of blank forms of writs and pleadings cannot resist the pressure of real life, and as the tract is edited and re-edited, first one redactor and then another puts in some actual case which has come within his knowledge. Eventually, the fascination of real cases will be so strong that at least one compiler who started out to copy a late version of *Brevia Placitata*

---

[1] Translated from *Brevia Placitata*, p. 21.
[2] Including 'a marvellous case' when a lord distrained two horses, of which one killed the other: *Brevia Placitata*, pp. 207–9.

abandoned that tract about a quarter of the way through and continued it without a break with some hundreds of pages of reports. That manuscript is in the Earl of Leicester's collection at Holkham.[1]

These indications of the future importance of cases concern principally the later rescensions, and we must return for one last look at the *Brevia Placitata* as it was originally put together around 1260. We must remember its French dress, its elementary character, its complete lack of arrangement—in short, its rudimentary, archaic air, and its ostentatious refusal of everything which Bracton stood for. Bracton addressed a class of lawyer-scholars who appreciated his cosmopolitan learning; *Brevia Placitata* addressed the thrusting young men who were too impatient to bother with the *Institutes*, or even with any English equivalent of that work. Their teacher showed them his collection of model forms, and very soon the pupils started pushing ahead; they wanted something even more actual than forms. Within them was the urge to 'get down to cases', and that had a momentous future.

Meanwhile, even in its baldest state, *Brevia Placitata* was a useful book. Other books were modelled on it, notably a group of tracts on the conduct of seignorial courts, some of which Maitland edited for the Selden Society in his volume *The Court Baron*. We need not suppose (as he did) that they may have come from the author of *Brevia Placitata*: but we must admit that they come from the same environment, and that they were addressed to the same public.[2] Law and business were inseparable in all ranks of the profession. Bracton's revered master William Rayleigh was not only lawyer and judge, but an outstanding financier in the king's service. Others combined the law with advising great land owners and religious houses on the management of their estates. The humbler practitioners no doubt conducted a nondescript and miscellaneous practice which included the equivalent of police-court work (so to speak) and the keeping of manorial courts. The tracts on the *Court Baron* were admirably designed for their instruction, and the work itself was for centuries a recognized introduction to legal practice. It will be remembered that Francis North (later

[1] For another sort of accident which produced the same result, see Z. N. Brooke, *English Church and the Papacy*, p. 89.

[2] Of the texts printed by Maitland in *Court Baron*, the one marked I is associated with Robert Carpenter, and III with Sir John of Longueville—both of them laymen. He gives a list of some early editions, 3–4.

Lord Keeper Guilford) long before his call to the bar in 1661 was obtaining valuable experience as a court-keeper.[1]

A third tract which followed the pattern of *Brevia Placitata* and the *Court Baron* goes by the name of *Ple de la Corone*, the 'Pleas of the Crown'. Manuscripts of it are fairly numerous, but it has never been printed. The three together (often accompanied by *Carta Feodi*,[2] a collection of conveyancing precedents) evidently formed the basic education of common lawyers generally, and covered the ground of a large proportion of modest country practices.

Itself directly based upon the Register of Writs, *Brevia Placitata* in turn was the foundation of another work, perhaps the most popular in the Middle Ages. This was *Novae Narrationes*. It is now known that this work dates from Edward I and not from Edward III as was formerly supposed. Its plan (or lack of plan) clearly shows its descent. It omits the writs (which were by now easily available in the Registers) and concentrates on the pleadings. It is not elementary but goes out of its way to find every imaginable complication, and so it soon grew into a fairly bulky book. Like its parent, it sticks grimly to the details of practice and became pre-eminently a practitioner's book.[3]

The class of literature which we have so far examined has at least a certain coherence in that it nearly all descends from the Register of Writs. Consequently it does have the slight discipline of dealing with the forms of action one by one. If we call that primitive, there is another tract which can only be called primeval, for its plan is utter chaos. This is *Casus Placitorum*,[4] the date of which is very close to *Brevia Placitata*. Once again we have to deal with a tract with many aliases: *Cas de Demaundes*, *Casus Brevium*, *Casus Curie*, and so on. There are about a dozen variant titles but it is now known by that bestowed upon it, seemingly, by Woodbine. One word is constant in all the variety, however, and that is the word 'Cases'. There a warning is needed. Those cases are not cases in the modern English sense of the word; that is to say, they are not necessarily and essentially narratives of judicial proceedings. The word must be taken in its Roman sense (which the moral theologians or 'casuists' also used), namely, to mean a

---

[1] Roger North, *Lives of the Norths* (1826), I, 33.
[2] There are numerous old editions from [1506] onwards.
[3] An edition for the Selden Society is in preparation by Miss Elsie Shanks.
[4] An edition for the Selden Society by Professor Dunham appeared in 1950.

set of circumstances, a state of facts. As we all know, 'circumstances alter cases'—change one material circumstance, and you
necessarily get a different case; those are the sort of 'cases' which
Casus Placitorum invites us to consider.

It has already been suggested that *Brevia Placitata* is an instructional work. That is even more the case with *Casus Placitorum*
which positively reeks of chalk and duster and ink. There is no
other work on English law which gives us so strong an impression
of being in a medieval class-room. It is much to be hoped that it
will catch the eye of some expert in teaching methods during the
Middle Ages, for he may be able to give a more precise meaning
to some of the technical words of the teacher's art which frequently
appear in it. In several of the titles given to the work it is described as *Cas e Demands* or *Cas de Demandes*. I have already put
forward a suggestion as to what the 'cases' were; but what were
the *Demandes*? One's first thought is of the demandant in the real
actions, and one is tempted to connect the *demandes* with those
encoupements or counts which the demandant so carefully frames
after the models in *Brevia Placitata*. If that were so, then *Casus
Placitorum* would be an exact translation of *Cas de Demandes*;
certainly some of the later versions took it that way, for they
allege the judgments of the king's justices upon these cases.
Judging from the earlier versions, it may well be that later copyists
(by this time familiar with the study of reported cases) misunderstood the word. For indubitably it is frequently used in the text,
not of a demand by a litigant, but of a question by a teacher, who
puts a *case* and *demands* an answer.[1] This sense long remained.
Books of jokes and funny stories might still be entitled *Demands
Joyous* (1509) or *Book of Demands* (after 1536).[2] This leads us to
another heuristic technicality: many items in *Casus Placitorum* are
labelled 'Aprise'. Professor Dunham, who had the difficult task
of translating this work, renders 'aprise' by 'rule'. This is possibly
as near as one can get with a single word. After the discussion in
class a conclusion is reached, which is more or less what we should
call a rule; but the word 'aprise' suggests (at least to my mind)
something more immediate: the conclusion reached is the thing
that the student must learn. The rubric 'aprise' seems to say
remember the discussion if you can, but *learn* this. However that

---

[1] For a case followed by a demand, see *Year Books of Edward II* (Selden
Society), XXIV, 133.   [2] *Short-Title Catalogue*, nos. 6572, 6573, 3188a.

may be, there is no denying that these words are part of the technical vocabulary of the teacher. The same spirit finally infected the later rescensions of *Brevia Placitata*, as is apparent from the late Harvard text.

Both tracts pursue a method of teaching by means of cases, but it is essential to distinguish that method from what is called the 'case method' of our own day. The modern method takes shape in *Smith's Leading Cases in the Common Law* (1837) and White and Tudor's *Leading Cases in Equity* (1849). They proceed from the assumption that the law can be deduced from the case, and expressed in the form of a commentary upon cases. The student is therefore invited to study the case and draw conclusions of law from it. Our tracts take the opposite view. The teacher is constantly putting cases to his pupils whose business it is to apply to the case such rules of law as they already know. In other words, we must compare these cases with a modern examination paper, not with a modern report.

Such then are the cases and demands and 'aprises' of our tract. It is they which seem to lie behind nearly everything in it, even when some of the steps are left out, and we get only the conclusion which is in many cases a succession of short paragraphs numbering less than one hundred in the earliest forms, but expanded to over two hundred in a few manuscripts. As I have said, the arrangement is different in all the manuscripts, which resemble one another only in being each of them chaotic. Nevertheless, there is a fairly large core of common material appearing in all of them, and that is the sole indication that our manuscripts, with all their divergencies, have a common ancestry and that they do represent to some extent a specific collection of material. The common ancestor may be a manuscript, but more probably (I think) the lessons of some anonymous teacher.

Occasionally the statements in *Casus Placitorum* give the name of a judge as warrant, and every one of these judges named in the earliest versions had retired or died by 1260. In the course of the 1250's, therefore, people were remembering notable sayings of the judges, among whom Thurkelby seems to have been conspicuously quotable. For example—

It is lawful for any man who has a franchise to put his villein in the stocks, but not to put him in prison. Witness Simon of Walton.[1]

---

[1] *Casus Placitorum* (Selden Society), 4, no. 16.

The writ of entry does not run for a remoter time than the writ of mort dancestor. Witness William of York.[1]

No one should say that a man is waived, but that a woman is waived and a man outlawed. Witness Roger of Thurkelby.[2]

Judges no doubt on suitable occasions 'laid down the law' on points which had been doubtful, and called attention to details which the lawyers present recognized as important. Such *dicta* from the bench would be remembered, not as cases are remembered now, but as the notable sayings of men in high office. There is evidence that this judicial habit was no novelty in the middle of the thirteenth century. Fifty years before the days of the *Casus* there are remarks in the rolls of Simon of Pateshall which his clerk (possibly the Martin of Pateshall who lived to become Bracton's hero) recorded, for in the reign of John the plea roll had not yet been reduced to the severely formal record it later became. In editing those rolls Lady Stenton commented upon these statements of legal rules in general terms;[3] now that the *Casus Placitorum* is in print they become all the more significant. Can we not say that, among the types of legal expression in England, we can discern an aphoristic tradition as old as the year 1202, perhaps even going back to the *Leges Henrici Primi*?[4] Such a tradition is not without parallel. The Digest itself concludes with the *De Regulis Juris*, and so does the Sext of Boniface VIII—and both collections of aphorisms, we may add, are as chaotic in arrangement as the *Casus*.

There is a teasing point which may be mentioned in conclusion. Bracton tells us much of certain judges who lived in the generation before his; of his own colleagues and contemporaries he maintains a contemptuous silence. Those colleagues may not have won the esteem of old Bracton, but they certainly impressed themselves on the younger generation, and if we are to estimate their quality we must read *Casus Placitorum*, *Brevia Placitata* and some of the other specimens of that group of tracts. Future commentators on Bracton—and his silences—will find much to their purpose in the *Casus*.

---

[1] *Casus Placitorum*, 5, no. 22.   [2] *Ibid.* 9, no. 41.

[3] *The Earliest Lincolnshire Assize Rolls* (ed. D. M. Stenton), xxiii.

[4] Anglo-Saxon law had a fondness for rhymes, jingles and the like; see the examples of rhyme, rhythm, assonance, alliteration, etc. discussed in F. E. Harmer, *Anglo-Saxon Writs*, pp. 85 ff.

Coming to these small tracts after reading Bracton produces something of a shock as we leave the splendour of the master's work and approach the squalid, disorderly little tracts where nothing seems to count except points of practice. Jurisprudence is indeed in total eclipse, and even literary form in its most rudimentary stage completely absent. The only concession to minds a little above the clay is when the compiler makes his point in the form of a riddle.

In what case can a minor recover his mother's heritage and yet his father not hold it for life by the curtesy?....[1]

In what case can a man admit he is a thief and have the stolen ox before him in full county court, and yet not be liable to be hanged by judgment?....[2]

That sort of thing bears the same relation to law as a crossword puzzle does to literature. And yet it is not to be altogether neglected. Trivial as it is, it is a bit better than the dull succession of paragraphs marked 'aprise'—'learn this bit' (which nowadays would be printed in black type for the guidance of the undiscerning dullard).

The new sort of law students for whom these works were prepared, like their teachers, seem to have been thoroughly philistine, deliberately cut-off from the universities and from the Roman and clerical traditions which the universities fostered. They chose instead to immerse themselves in these graceless tracts, written in the vulgar tongue, so as to prepare themselves for a rude profession where wits rather than scholarship were in demand.

And yet among this hard-bitten crowd there were a few who had in some mysterious way received the grace of scholarship, and who set themselves the task of presenting the law in a way which would satisfy the intellect. If that could be done, English law would be saved, and saved without Bracton—for the new generation of lawyers would have nothing of him. It is true that numerous copies of Bracton at this very moment were being made, but those manuscripts have an unmistakably monastic look. They were surely read in many an abbey, but it is rare indeed to find one with the French marginal notes of a man of affairs (such as the famous

---

[1] *Casus Placitorum*, 9, no. 40, which vouches H. de Bath for the answer.
[2] *Ibid.* 35, no. 1.

but still unprinted Longueville gloss); and no one who reads only the Year Books would ever suspect that Bracton had lived and written. Indeed, the persistent tradition that Bracton is not a 'book of authority' tells its own story.

If Bracton was to be abandoned, two possible courses were open. One was to abridge his book—and that gave us Hengham, *Fleta*, Thornton, and the French version in Britton. The other, the heroic way, was to start again right at the beginning and work out afresh the logical framework of English law, and to state its principles in the vernacular language of the English courts. The one or two brave and able men who tackled this problem have left no names behind them, but only their books. Tiny books indeed, but books evidently written with a breadth of mind which has won the respect of at least one modern reader; books which were, unhappily, too good for their public and left no posterity.

The outstanding member of this group is *Fet Asaver*, whose merits have been too long obscured by his editors. A few pages of this work were printed by accident at the end of Selden's edition of *Fleta* in 1647. The only complete edition is by Woodbine who does much less than justice to the *Four Tracts* which he brought out in 1910. It is the shortcomings of that edition which are evidently responsible for the failure to recognize the quality of *Fet Asaver*. The text is itself unsound in places, and too often obscured by wrong punctuation which breaks up the author's sentences. The lack of a translation leaves the reader to cope unaided with very technical matter couched in a peculiar dialect, and its omission allowed textual errors to pass which would certainly have been cleared up if the editor had been under the salutary discipline of translating his text. There are no indications given of the places where this and the other authors have borrowed from Bracton or even from the statutes. Since there is no table of contents or tabular analysis of the several tracts, their structure is not revealed—indeed it is obscured, for the editor has failed to set out the subdivisions of the texts, even when they are plainly indicated by the author. Add to that the lack of an index, and it will be appreciated that any reader who wishes to make a serious study of the tracts will have to undertake a good deal of editorial work before he begins.

Fet Asaver opens with a sentence which demands serious consideration. 'All pleas in the king's court', we are told, 'are either pleas of land, or of trespass, or both.' Taking pleas of land first, they are of four sorts only, being based on

> fee, and demesne and right; or
> fee and right without demesne; or
> fee and demesne without right; or
> demesne without fee or right.

After reading *Brevia Placitata* and *Casus Placitorum*, one can hardly forbear to cheer an author who gets all that into his first eighty words. Here at last is a man who has thought about law and the English system of remedies as a whole, who can construct a general proposition and analyse it into its branches.[1]

This is not the occasion for a full discussion of this analysis, which would carry us far into the field of actions and of substantive property law. The point immediately before us is the achievement of our new legal profession. One or two of its members have succeeded in starting afresh on the endless task of framing an intellectual system out of the native materials of English law, and have succeeded in reaching a result of considerable originality.

That can be seen at once by contrasting these opening words of *Fet Asaver* with Bracton ff. 159b–60. Both were faced with the problem of where to begin, and how to proceed, in a discussion of the English forms of action. Bracton unhesitatingly went to the fountain-head of legal theory, the Romanists, and produced the scheme of dividing all actions into civil or criminal; all civil actions into real or personal; and all real actions into proprietary or possessory. Then possession is further discussed in terms of vestments and cause. As everyone knows, these foreign categories did not entirely fit our system of actions, and Bracton had difficulties. He was not sure whether he should classify novel disseisin as real or personal;[2] his possession does not square with the real facts of English law which rested not upon the classical possession but upon seisin. All the same Bracton's great merit is to have shown for the first time that English law *ought* to be studied analytically;

---

[1] It is not suggested that this necessarily came in a flood of illumination; it is possible that the idea may have developed from the notion expressed in *Casus Placitorum*, 4, no. 19.

[2] Bracton regarded novel disseisin as a personal action on ff. 103b–104, but as a real action on f. 159b.

the merit of *Fet Asaver* is to have shown for the first time how it could be *done* in purely native terms.[1]

And so once more English law in the pages of *Fet Asaver* becomes the object of serious thought instead of a mere conglomeration of procedural technicalities. On the merits, the author of *Fet Asaver* deserves the highest praise, for it was he, more than anyone else, who 'turned his eyes away from the glittering pages of the Digest' and struck out an original line of thought of his own.

Nor was he the only one. On a lower plane the author of the *Modus Componendi Brevia*[2] was also applying an acute mind to legal problems. He approaches the matter from the point of view of a practitioner interviewing a client, who has to decide, after hearing the client's story,[3] what remedy is open to him. His method is dialectic, and by following it the right remedy ought to emerge. In terms, it is purely a practical method of handling a problem in the lawyer's daily round of work; but he also has thought logically about the writ system, and the result is a classification of remedies. He has the merit of frankly basing everything upon seisin instead of attempting the analysis of rights which *Fet Asaver* undertook. The practitioner naturally starts with seisin, for it is the most conspicuous fact in a case—at least when he hears it for the first time from a client. Indeed, seisin goes more deep than that, for it is around seisin rather than around rights that the law took shape in the course of the preceding centuries. The *Modus* goes further than *Fet Asaver* in one respect, for it defines a 'plea of land'; the author does not discuss the difficulties he encountered, but he must have pondered them at length before he reached finally the definition that a plea of land is one in which the great and petty *cape* are part of the process; all other actions are 'trespass' in which the process is by grand distress. In abandoning Bracton's real-and-personal scheme, the author therefore acted deliberately and had his reason ready. His own scheme is this: Actions of land

---

[1] *Fet Asaver* concludes (pp. 112–15 in Woodbine's *Four Tracts*) with a section on trespass in which he includes debt 'or other like sorts of tort'. This is reminiscent of the 'wrangous' detention of a debt, etc. mentioned by Lord Cooper, *The Dark Age of Scottish Legal History*, 19. Cf. Ernst Levy, *West Roman Vulgar Law* (Philadelphia, 1951), I, 241, and Pollock and Maitland, *History of English Law*, II, 206 for the English use of 'deforce'.

[2] In Woodbine, *Four Tracts*, pp. 143 ff.; here too pleas are either 'of land' or 'of trespass'.

[3] 'Audito casu conquerentis, videatur si actio sit realis...', Woodbine, *Four Tracts*, p. 144.

are brought in two ways. First, on the demandant's own seisin; this he will have lost (*a*) because he has been disseised, or (*b*) because he alienated, for example for a term of years, or while he was under age, etc. Alternatively, the action may be based on the seisin of the demandant's ancestor with four possibilities: (*a*) that the ancestor died seised, or (*b*) he died disseised, or (*c*) he had alienated, or (*d*) a doweress had alienated.

All that is worked out with considerable detail and ingenuity, and, in general, writs fall into place quite easily. The history of these various schemes for classifying rights, or remedies, has much importance for the general history of English law, but in the present context we have to consider it only as part of the endeavour to make the law rational and systematic. That the young legal profession should have produced two such attempts as these is very much to its credit. If the effort had been continued, then indeed old Bracton could have rested content that his great work had served its purpose nobly, and that younger men were thinking keenly, and in his spirit, even although it was along very different lines.

The event proved otherwise. By the death of Edward I this wave of scholarship in the vernacular had spent its force, and the fourteenth-century lawyer is brought up henceforth on forms alone—on the unscientific works which derived ultimately from the Register, especially *Novae Narrationes*, and the old *Natura Brevium*. These, with the Register and the statutes, supplied such mental discipline as his teachers could devise. There was one development only; the cases which constituted a part of the old *Casus Placitorum*, *Brevia Placitata*, and the rest, could be modernized. Real cases were collected. Not authoritative cases like the decretals, and not digested into a *corpus juris* such as the canonists were building up, but just cases, almost any cases that turned up. Chance alone determined the contents of any particular collection, and every vestige of a scientific approach to law disappeared. The lawyers accepted the return of chaos cheerfully and have long ago got used to it.

CHAPTER VI

CASES AND YEAR BOOKS

TWICE in the thirteenth century attempts were made to express English law in a systematic, rational, scientific form. First it was Bracton who employed the resources of the Roman and canonist masters to produce a book, in Latin, addressed to English lawyers who had been brought up in the clerical tradition and expected a law-book to be built upon the plan of contemporary civilian and canonical works. That public was rapidly being replaced by another whose tastes were very different. The academic Roman, Latin and clerical tradition had no attractions for the new men who were insular, French and lay, and who were nevertheless destined to be the foundation of the legal profession in England. The new French legal literature indeed shows, in its first vigorous youth, several attempts to devise its own scholarly technique of dealing with the law, and high praise must be given to the authors of *Fet Asaver* and *Modus Componendi Brevia*. At least the elect among the new-comers had caught the idea of legal scholarship, and saw English law as a logical scheme of remedies, and even of rights.

For a time they impressed themselves upon their contemporaries, and manuscripts of *Fet Asaver* are fairly numerous. It was too good to last. The increasing bulk of the plea rolls under Edward I and Edward II seems to betoken a flood of litigation, and (from other sources) we learn also of a flood of entrants into legal practice. There must have been some degree of 'dilution', and standards fell. Instead of proceeding from *Fet Asaver* to fresh feats of legal analysis, we fell far behind.

The situation can best be judged from the books which grew, and the books which declined. *Fet Asaver* after a brief moment of popularity seems to lose ground and by the end of the fourteenth century seems out of use. The fact that it was not printed under Henry VIII shows that it had passed out of lawyers' minds by then. Britton had a vogue under the first three Edwards and was printed in 1542, evidently because it was the only work to deal with the legislation of Edward I, however summarily. But the books which really survived as living sources of instruction were

not the treatises but the formularies. The Register of Writs necessarily assumed monstrous proportions and in due course was
printed, but at no time had its primitive form been reduced to
order. Similarly, the *Novae Narrationes* became a sizeable book,
constantly recopied and eventually printed, but retaining its
disorderly form until the end.

The one new departure, which in time was to overshadow all
the older literature, consisted in the collecting of cases. In one
sense of that word Englishmen had been ardent collectors of cases
for over a century before the Year Books began to appear;[1]
already in the time of Glanvill, English canonists displayed their
foible for collecting when, from about 1175 onwards, they compiled
collections of papal decretals with which to supplement the *Decretum* of Gratian, now a generation old. In this enterprise they took
the initiative,[2] although it is only to be expected that Continental
collectors should soon outstrip them since they had many more
decretals to collect.

It is easy to see why decretals should have been collected.
Important cases in canon law were tried by judges delegate, and,
when the delegates were confronted with difficult questions of law,
they referred those questions to Rome. The answer came back in the
form of a decretal letter in which the highest authority of the
church resolved the problem. At first, no doubt, that decision was
absolutely binding only in the case which gave rise to it, but very
soon it was apparent that the highest respect was due to decretals
as authoritative pronouncements from Rome upon the points of
law.

The position of the English courts was not so very different.
Bracton himself makes the point that the justices of the court of
common pleas are in effect judges delegate because they exercise
a jurisdiction not their own but delegated to them by the king,[3]
and from the plea rolls we can see that they sometimes consulted
the king and his council in the course of difficult cases, asking for
directions upon doubtful points of law. The king, like the pope,
gave them an authoritative answer which they applied to the case
before them. The only difference was that the pope necessarily

[1] S. Kuttner and E. Rathbone, 'Anglo-Norman canonists', *Traditio*, VII,
279 ff.
[2] This seems to explain the conspicuous number of English cases in the
Decretals which Maitland observed: Pollock and Maitland, *History of English
Law*, I, 115.   [3] Bracton, f. 108.

had to write letters in order to communicate with his far-flung delegates scattered all over Christendom; the king on the other hand was within easy reach (either personally or by his council) and could instruct his delegates without the solemnity of a decretal.[1] This trivial circumstance set our judicial procedure upon a different course from that of the church, for there were no documents to collect. When common lawyers began to report cases they had to be content with something much less imposing than royal decretals.

Besides the canon law, there are other legal systems which merit attention if we are to make a comparative survey of the position of cases as a source of law in the Middle Ages. In particular, the law of Normandy lies very close to us for reasons that are obvious. The social habits, the feudal framework and the judicial organization of the duchy are very closely related to our own. Like us, Normandy had a system of actions based upon original writs and a method of pleading and procedure which any reader of Bracton or the Year Books would recognize as familiar. Like us, moreover, Normandy produced several collections of cases which deserve attention.

The Norman lawyers, like many of their fellows in other French jurisdictions, soon perceived that cases were not all of the same legal weight, and so they undertook a rough classification of decisions. The ordinary case decided in the usual way and calling for no particular attention was described in the collections as 'jugé', 'judicatum'.[2] There were others, however, where judgment was not given immediately but reserved until the end of term, when the court sat as a council and resolved its doubts. Clearly such decisions given after mature deliberation seemed particularly important to practitioners, and they were assiduously collected under the name of 'arrêts', 'arresta' or 'notables'.

Moreover, a Norman court, like an English one, would sometimes take the occasion of a particular case to make a general ruling. Such quasi-legislative decisions were called (in the fourteenth century in Normandy) 'atiramenta', 'atirements', and they too were collected by practitioners.

Yet another type of decision was concerned with the proof of

---

[1] For a very rare exception, see *Hapeton's Case* which became the 'statute of waste': *Rotuli Parliamentorum*, I, 79, no. 6; *Statutes of the Realm*, I, 109.

[2] Cf. R. Génestal and J. Tardif, *Atiremens et Jugiés d'Eschequiers* (Caen, 1921), pp. xxiv ff.

custom. Where the parties and the advocates of a court agreed upon the existence of a custom, the court would hold it for 'notorious'—and practitioners would make a note of it. So too if the custom were disputed, for then the solemn mode of proof by inquest would be invoked.[1]

It is obvious therefore that if cases are to be studied at all, due regard must be had to their classification, from which it results inevitably that only certain decisions, reached by certain procedures, could be considered as authoritative statements of law. Another element in the situation is the relationship between bench and bar, and the structure of the court. Therein lies the explanation of the startling ordinance of the Norman exchequer dated 23 June 1454 which prohibited law-reporting in that court.[2] The exchequer had in fact retained its ancient constitution whereby the bystanders (notably the advocates) participated in reaching the judgment. The court evidently disliked the possibility of setting up the opinions of eminent practioners in opposition to the decision of the court and therefore forbade the practice of reporting them.

The Norman collections are older than most of ours, for several of them contain material going back to 1207. Like ours they are of two sorts: those derived from the record of the court, and those derived from hearing the oral proceedings.

It is in the light of these contemporary practices that we must approach the problem of English law-reporting, for the significance of what was happening in England will best appear when it is compared with what other lawyers were doing in other jurisdictions. Making that comparison, it is at once evident that there are similarities, but many more differences. In England, as in Normandy, there were in the thirteenth century collections based upon court records. Bracton's *Note Book* is by far the largest example, but there were others.[3] Likewise, such collections might consist of full transcripts, or of short summaries; they might also be general and miscellaneous, or be confined to cases of particular actions—the petty assizes were a favourite sort to collect.

---

[1] On 'notables' and 'coutumes notoires' see Olivier Martin, *Histoire de la coutume... de Paris*, I, 82 ff.; cf. the chapter by Viollet, 'Recueils de jurisprudence normande', *Histoire littéraire de la France*, XXXIII, 174–90, and E. Perrot, 'Décisions de jurisprudence normande', *Revue historique de droit français* [1911].

[2] R. Besnier, *La Coutume de Normandie*, pp. 117–18.

[3] For example, *Casus et Judicia*, printed in *Casus Placitorum* (ed. Dunham, Selden Society), lxxv–lxxxix.

The collections based upon oral reporting in court, on both sides of the Channel, are frequently indifferent to personal and local details. In both cases the report may take the form of a brief narrative of the proceedings,[1] but in England there developed very soon a strong tendency to cast the report into dialogue form. Thus proper names become frequent, but they are the names of the serjeants, not of the parties. Eventually that became the characteristic type of English law report, and in due course the Year Books became essentially memorials of the great leaders of the bar in their contests with one another and in their relation to the bench. Occasionally a Continental report is in dialogue, but it is very rare. The names of famous advocates also figure largely in some types of Continental collection, but obviously for different reasons. Constituting, as they did, a part of the court, their opinions carried weight by themselves and so were collected; our English courts on the other hand were so dominated by the bench that the serjeants are clearly regarded as contestants before the judges, who appraise their performance with an expert eye.

It is that state of affairs which produced the greatest divergences between English and Continental law-reporting. The Continental reporter is consciously engaged in collecting authorities, decisions which tell him unmistakably the rules of law. Every case in his book is decided—in the rare instances when there is no decision an editor can only conclude that at that date the author broke off his work unfinished. It is notorious, however, that our Year Books (and their forerunners) seem indifferent to the decision, and that a high proportion of cases are reported without judgments.

If we couple this circumstance with those already noted—the strong tendency to dialogue, and the prominence of the serjeants —it becomes clear that, in general, our English reporters are not primarily looking for 'authority', still less for substantive law. If they had been, they would have cut short the debates, extracted the point of law, and concentrated upon the decision and the reasons for it. Moreover, they would have devised some scheme of distinguishing important decisions from merely routine judgments upon the ordinary run of cases which inevitably constituted most of a court's daily work. The fact that they did not do so shows clearly that their minds were directed to other matters.

[1] A good example is 'Notes d'audience prises au Parlement de Paris, 1384–6', *Revue historique de droit* [1923], pp. 513 ff.

Their great preoccupation, I believe, was pleading and procedure. The common law remained until the end of the Middle Ages in a singularly backward state in both of these subjects. Procedure on the Continent had been studied with great eagerness and large masses of learning had been assembled as civilians and canonists applied themselves to Justinian's books, and attempted to import the results into the native customary or national laws. In the slow process of rationalization, procedure came to be more and more separated from substantive law. In England, on the other hand, procedure resisted all foreign attacks. Bracton with all his admiration for Roman and canon developments made no attempt to express English procedure in romanesque language. He made valiant efforts to separate our substantive law from its procedural entanglements, but in the end he had to leave our procedure as he found it—the original writs, the common-law actions, the famous 'delays' (which were almost a sacred birthright of English litigants) he could describe in minute detail, but to modify them was beyond the realm of possibility.

Pleading was a part of that complex mass of technicality. Many Continental systems welcomed the efforts of canonists and civilians to ascertain the legal issues of a case before it came into court, so that the court could concentrate on deciding the case. Once again, Bracton did not venture to recommend that scientific and enlightened course. We retained our antique system, under which a case was submitted to the judges who had no inkling of what it was about, beyond what could be gathered from the original writ. The whole process of analysing the case, in order to ascertain what the parties were fighting about, had to take place in open court. The facts of a case were a jealously guarded secret which was revealed to the court grudgingly and under pressure. Many a time our reports show us the bench protesting that counsel are 'pleading covertly' and that they can make neither head nor tail of the affair.

The whole business of pleading orally, in face of the court and with opponents ready to pounce at any moment, was an immensely skilful and recondite game, conducted with great virtuosity by the leaders of the bar, and keenly relished by all others who were sufficiently learned to understand what it was all about. After such a display, it was an anti-climax to think of a decision. Time after time the Year Books will give pages of subtle fencing until we get the words: 'and so to judgment'. What the judgment was, nobody knew and nobody cared; what interested the reader was not the substantive law involved in a case, but the technique of conducting the pleadings so as to produce, if possible, a satisfactory issue of law or fact.

Necessarily, that made the use of cases as an authority of law well-nigh impossible. Our earliest and simplest reports, it is true, resemble Continental models. They start with a statement of facts and give us an indication of the law which will apply. But that is only for elementary students. As the system develops it becomes evident that what the public wants is choice examples of forensic fencing by the most admired masters.

The contrast with Bracton's *Note Book* is noticeable. The early cases which he selected from the plea rolls antedate the elaborate development of the system; after Bracton's day selections from the plea rolls gradually ceased to interest practitioners just because the roll did not recount the really exciting part of the story, but merely the pleadings as ultimately enrolled.

The changes which were to set our legal science upon a new course were not decided upon in a day, nor was it immediately clear in what direction English law would develop. The fateful years in the middle of the thirteenth century were full of possibilities, no doubt, but a possibility is itself an uncertainty. Bracton was laying aside his great work unfinished: who could say at that moment whether his massive volume would turn the scale and make English legal practice Roman, Latin and clerical? *Fet Asaver* was soon to appear: who could venture the guess that it would make our law vernacular and lay, but still strongly analytic in its native way? *Brevia Placitata* and *Casus Placitorum* were already taking shape (if we can talk of shape in connexion with such shapeless works): but was there a pessimist sufficiently despondent to foretell that the future of English law lay in those miserable little tracts? If there had been, he would have been right, but his fore-knowledge would have been miraculous.

The great political and constitutional issues of the period of the Barons' Wars have been studied with immense care by many historians, and they agree that the legal aspect of those events is an essential part of the general story; and yet the legal history of the period is still incompletely explored. The breadth and lucidity of Maitland's *History of English Law* is partly the product of Maitland's own clear vision, but it is also the reflexion in some measure of Bracton's as well. Maitland's great work is essentially Bractonian. As we have seen, however, Bracton was not the only force at work, and certainly not the finally decisive one, in the formation of the classical common law. Maitland knew that, and had he been spared the normal span of life he would have explored the non-Bractonian elements as well. Already in 1891 he was turning the pages of *Brevia Placitata* and setting G. J. Turner to edit it. He realized the capital importance of the Year Books and spent his last days editing them. Above all, he discerned the crucial problem of the earliest reports of cases, sought manuscripts of them, and transcribed a very bulky collection which unhappily has not yet been published—through the remissness of Turner, who has left among his papers his confession of the fact.

Maitland has clearly indicated the direction of the next step: the earliest collections of cases must be discovered, dated, edited and studied, not only for the law which they contain, but also as collections—as the physical evidence left behind them by men who were studying or teaching or practising law. It is only when we know why and how and when those cases were reported or collected that we can surmise what lay in lawyers' minds upon such matters as the source of English law, and the nature of the authority upon which an exposition of English law would have to rest.

The task is difficult and laborious, but already something has been accomplished. Professor W. H. Dunham has enriched his edition of *Casus Placitorum* by adding to it two collections of cases from the early years of Edward I, which deserve careful study, and also a collection of notes headed 'Casus et judicia'[1] which contains cases dated between 1252 and 1256. This is our earliest known collection (after *Bracton's Note Book*) and, like some similar works on the Continent, is derived (in part at least) from the plea rolls, to which it gives express references. It is in Latin like *Bracton's Note Book*, but does not give a transcript of the roll, only a summary. It is very well done by a compiler who had a clear idea of what he wanted; he extracted the point of his cases with skill and precision, and took care to give us the judgment. The original work is lost; the manuscript which has come down to us is in a good hand, well written, but badly copied. Interspersed with the cases from the plea rolls are short statements of legal principle for which no cases are cited. For this some copyist is doubtless responsible, or some

---

[1] Dunham, *Casus Placitorum* (Selden Society, vol. LXIX), lxxv.

interpolator. The dated cases do not occur in chronological order, nor is the work as a whole in any systematic order; so it would seem that a variety of hands have meddled with the original collection, without, however, obscuring the fact that the ultimate compiler was a competent lawyer who steadily saw the law and expressed it clearly and succinctly with the plea rolls before his eyes.

The two Edwardian collections[1] just mentioned introduce us into an entirely different world. It is the world of French, instead of Latin, writing, and the source of the material is not the plea roll but the oral exchanges in court. Consequently its origin lies in reporting. In the main, both collections are very similar in style; both of them contain a slight amount of material which is in the form of didactic notes, but the large majority of the items are cases reported in dialogue form. Occasionally the dialogue is attributed to the parties, but in general it is the counsel whose names precede each speech. The cases are really choice; every one of them raises important legal points and the report makes them easily visible. We cannot escape drawing the conclusion: their compiler was an able and experienced man—he could not have assembled so many good cases unless he had spent some years collecting, for they are by no means the usual run of the mill—and finally, he must have edited them to some extent. This last point is important, for we can see from the Year Books of the next reign how tentative much of the debate was, before the counsel on either side finally settled how the case was to be pleaded. It is quite different with these two early collections; there is no discursiveness or repetition, for the dialogue immediately, and without preliminaries, goes straight to the legal point. Furthermore, some of the reports are introduced by a statement of the facts without reporting the tedious process of eliciting those facts in the course of the case. In short, these two collections covering several years are careful selections of very choice cases, and skilfully edited so as to make clear the legal points involved. If we were to settle down to a system of case literature, these two collections showed one way of doing it; but clearly its success depended upon a good deal of thoughtful work by an able lawyer.

Now consider the implications of that. The skilfully compressed version which has come down to us could only have been prepared from a fuller, rougher version from which the editor cut out

[1] *Casus Placitorum*, pp. 45, 86.

superfluous matter. Even the rougher version may not have been the first. Further, the manuscript which has come down to us is a copy from a previous manuscript, for there is a conspicuous example of haplography on page 58 of the first collection. Again, both these collections contain a few cases of which reports are to be found in other manuscripts so we must postulate either independent reporters, or else a very complicated manuscript history behind the surviving texts (and probably both suppositions may be true). Lastly, the great similarity in style and competence may indicate that both collections come from the same source. And yet for the most part both manuscripts are unique, as far as is known at present.

It would be hazardous at this stage to conclude anything at all definite about the process by which the original first report has come down to us in these manuscripts, save that the process was certainly complicated, and that at some point (probably, but not necessarily, an early point) some skilled and sensible lawyer spent a good deal of trouble and care in editing rough material, and putting it into the shape which has come down to us.

On the other hand, the process by which the original first report came into existence is now within our range of knowledge, thanks to an important discovery by Professor Dunham of certain slips of parchment[1] used to strengthen the binding of the manuscript Stowe 386 in the British Museum. These are irregularly shaped scraps of parchment, two of which contain French reports of cases in small, hasty writing with many cancellations and interlineations. One of the slips contains, besides a report, some miscellaneous matter—notably some satiric verses on the famous purge of the judicial bench by Edward I in the years around 1290. A third slip professes to be a transcript of a plea roll of 1306.

The discovery of these slips confirms what was already a very probable surmise,[2] namely, that a report necessarily begins with the rough note made in court at (or immediately after) the hearing. Evidently that rough note would be made on a small scrap of parchment left over from something else, for parchment was very costly. (Even the chancery itself issued original writs on narrow ribbons of parchment of all shapes and sizes bearing minute writing

---

[1] *Ibid.* xc.
[2] As early as 1910 Dr Bolland had suggested the use of 'odd scraps of parchment': *Eyre of Kent* (Selden Society), i, xcix.

tightly crowded upon a singularly inadequate surface.[1]) It is such rough notes which necessarily lie behind the fair copies, expanded and edited, which come down to us in book form.

Evidently, the editorial work was best done by the original reporter while the case was fresh in his memory. But it was not necessarily so. There are reports in the Year Books which contain errors of law which hitherto have been difficult to explain—mishandling and mis-citing of statutes, for example. Professor Dunham's discovery leads me to think that possibly such solecisms may be the work of an editor expanding another man's notes of a case which he did not hear, and whose nature he mistook.

The process of editing introduces different considerations. The man who undertakes it does so in order to give some measure of permanence as well as intelligibility to the raw material. He is unlikely to do this for a single case, and naturally the result of his labours is not a case, but a collection of cases. The collection may be large or small, and it would be hazardous in the extreme to suppose that the editor was the author of all the rough notes which he used. Nor need we assume that one collection had only one editor; it may well have happened that the maker of some rough reports wrote them up by way of an addendum to, or enlargement of, a previously edited collection. So too, the rough notes, once they were edited, could be dealt with in various ways. They might become mere scrap (and we know now that such scrap might find its way into an old book-binding). On the other hand, the slips might come to the hands of another lawyer who would himself prepare an independent edition of them and put them (perhaps mingled with others) into his own collection.

We have thus to consider the further point that these notes, when edited, normally take their place in a collection. The simplest and most natural situation is when a given bundle of slips is edited so as to become a single collection in a book. There is a good deal of variety among the early collections. Some are entirely miscellaneous. Others seem to relate all to one jurisdiction such as cases before justices in eyre. These clearly originate with reporters who followed the circuit of those justices, while the fact that in some manuscripts there is confusion between the eyre of Cornwall of 1303 and the eyre of Kent of 1313 suggests that some people

[1] A number of writs are illustrated by Lady Stenton in *Pleas before the King or his Justices* (Selden Society, vol. LXVII), plates V, VI and VII.

were interested in eyres as such;[1] it may even be possible that the manuscript situation is the result, not of conflating manuscripts, but of confusing slips. Other collections consist mainly or solely of petty assizes—either because these popular forms of action deserved special study, or (more probably) because the reporters were following the circuit of some judge of assize.

The point has often been debated: are these collections the work of lawyers or of students? Such debates are further embroiled by the fact that the ancestor of the modern barrister was officially described as an 'apprentice', who retained this humble designation until he entered the extremely select circle of the serjeants. It is hardly possible to be precise about this until the early organization of the legal profession has been more clearly ascertained. At present it seems that we must imagine the bulk of these men as 'pupil-teachers' and many of them as being of mature years and experience. What they did, and how they earned a living, we can hardly say. The Year Books, like the earlier reports, give us hardly any sign of their existence, and none whatever of their functions. Perhaps they acted as juniors to the serjeants who alone appear in the reports. The serjeants may have been conceived as being in a sense just as much members of the court, like their brethren in Normandy and elsewhere, as advocates of one of the parties. Certainly there is plenty of evidence late in the Middle Ages that the serjeants were associated with judges in deciding cases in the exchequer chamber, in serjeants' inn, and in chancery. In the present state of our knowledge it seems precarious to assume that there was a sharp line between learners and practitioners, between pupils and teachers. The notion of a pupil-teacher is ages older than the nineteenth century.

Fairly soon, in the closing years of Edward I, one type of collection becomes steadily more prominent until finally it is the normal, and indeed the universal, form. It represents the abandonment of any attempt at classification of cases by their subject-matter. The process of editing is less drastic, the legal point of the case is often less clearly brought out, and the often rambling and repetitive dialogue of the actual court proceedings seems reproduced with

---

[1] *Eyre of Kent* (ed. Bolland, Selden Society), I, pp. xcix, 102–34, where there are a number of cases already printed in *Year Books 30–1 Edward I* (ed. Horwood, Rolls Series), pp. 497–526. Woodbine noted (although he did not discover) the fact: book review, *Yale Law Journal*, XLVII, 1232.

more fidelity. The rough notes taken in court may perhaps have been rather fuller: in any case the editorial process seems to have been to expand them into dialogue which sounds extremely vivid and natural, rather than to prune a rambling debate of its irrelevancies so as to exhibit the points of the case. Above all, the very choice selections of really important cases, such as those edited by Professor Dunham, in which the cream of several years of reporting is presented in quite a small compass, yield place to bulkier collections whose unity is purely chronological. That fact is advertised by the headings, which consist of a date expressed in terms and regnal years. In other words, we simply get a Year Book, containing the year's cases (or the term's cases in some manuscripts).

Into all the multifarious problems presented by these fascinating productions it is quite impossible to enter on this occasion. We may ask why it should have been thought useful to have such full reports—why the cut-and-thrust of advocacy should be so laboriously recorded, why the personalities of Hervey 'the Hasty' and Chief Justice Bereford with his fearful oaths and stories, too blue for Maitland to translate, should be solemnly committed to fine parchment volumes. We are indeed profoundly grateful for these revelations, but why did fourteenth-century lawyers buy such books at a great price? Above all, why do manuscripts of them suddenly become very numerous for the first half of the reign of Edward II?

That last point is particularly teasing. It seems clearly connected with the sudden increase in the mass of business passing through the courts, and the increase in the number of lawyers which doubtless accompanied it. The suggestion that these Year Books were commercially produced is at first sight attractive, but the textual evidence is against it. Such a method would have produced longer units—possibly whole volumes. No one manuscript contains more than a fraction of the cases in any particular term, and there are many uncollatable versions of the same case. That is very different from a mass-produced report. When we remember that there may be more than a hundred cases a term reported, it is at once clear that the standard of collection has fallen, and that many slips of parchment which once would have never been made (or, if made, would have been abandoned) are now being embodied into formal collections. One can only conjecture why this should be: my own guess would attribute it to the combined effect of falling standards and a rapid increase in the number of young lawyers. The existence of many independent reporters may very well have resulted in a fairly brisk exchange of materials among lawyers, but here again we must remember that in some cases at least what changed hands may have been not finished manuscripts, but bundles of slips. Consequently, the textual situation is not quite the same as in purely literary texts, and manuscript relationships must be sought less in the order of the cases, and more in the constant appearance of particular cases in a group irrespective of their order within the group.

The extremely complex state of the Year Book text in the reign of Edward II is a problem by itself; the remarkably simple textual situation of the later Year Books is yet a different puzzle. Here the fewness of the manuscripts is as striking as their abundance was in the earlier period. Moreover, their unanimity of text leaves no room for any but the simplest sort of textual history. That is particularly true of the reign of Richard II; in the fifteenth century the few surviving manuscripts often contain among them some which are visibly abbreviations of the fuller report. The number of reported cases generally falls, and for some of the years there are no extant manuscripts, although early printed editions exist. Indeed, the text of the old prints may be markedly better than that of any surviving manuscripts. It is quite impossible to believe that there was any lively interest in the Year Books, or any serious desire to have cases reported, in the latter half of the fifteenth century. The practice of reporting and collecting cases survived, but only just. There are a few manuscripts which show that some readers pursued the ancient method of common-placing such cases as they found, and the early printed abridgments are merely exceptionally large examples, probably constructed by combining into one alphabet several smaller abridgments.[1]

The discovery of printing slowly wrought a change in this situation. Lawyers might risk a modest sum on a printed Year Book, although they would not face the expenditure of getting one in manuscript. Printers, who were sometimes at a loss to know what to print, experimented with a few Year Books and the result is very illuminating.

---

[1] For a manuscript which had been constructed in this way, see *Harvard Law Review*, XXXIX, 408. For evidence that Fitzherbert's *Abridgment* was constructed in the same way, see S. E. Thorne, 'Fitzherbert's Abridgment', *Law Library Journal*, XXIX, 59.

As far as is known, the experiment began when the firm of Lettou and Machlinia brought out the *Year Books 33–37 Henry VI* about the year 1481. In other words, cases decided between 1454 and 1459 were chosen for printing in 1481—at least twenty years later. What about the cases being decided in that year 1481? They were indeed printed, but not until 1520, some forty years later. Odd years of Edward IV's reign got into print at various dates down to 1499, and in 1502 some cases as recent as 1492 (only ten years old) came from the press. At the same time a volume of Edward III's Year Books came out, and from then onwards there was a flood of fourteenth-century cases coming from the sixteenth-century printers.

There immediately arises the question: why old cases? Why not current cases? There is real point in this, as will be seen when we look at the list of printed statutes. Thus we find that this same Machlinia printed, in 1484, the statutes of 1483. The next venture was by Caxton who printed the statutes of 1485–9 in that same year 1489. Thenceforward, the printers contrived to publish the new statutes shortly after the conclusion of the parliament that made them. Lawyers evidently supported these ventures steadily, and so the long series of session-laws was quickly established. Now observe that the fifteenth- and sixteenth-century printer was quite capable of getting out the latest statutes within a year of their enactment. Why did he wait on an average about thirty or forty years to bring out the latest cases? The answer must be that the profession did not want them. On the other hand, there was a fair market for Year Books of Edward III and the Lancastrian kings. The conclusion seems inescapable that old Year Books were found moderately useful (probably as material for study), but that recent cases had no particular attraction for lawyers.[1]

It was Tottel who organized the publication of Year Books, and it was he who standardized their pagination. He noted that the great Abridgment of Fitzherbert was selling well, so he brought out a new edition with cross-references to his Year Books; then he reprinted many Year Books with cross-references to his Fitzherbert. No doubt he told the profession that a set of Tottels was indispensable. Everything conspires to suggest that for the first time since Edward II lawyers were beginning to take Year Books

---

[1] Coke himself only discovered this slowly: T. F. T. Plucknett, 'The Genesis of Coke's Reports', *Cornell Law Quarterly*, XXVII, 190–213.

seriously—thanks to the acumen of Tottel. Other law-books came to be decorated with references to the Year Books, in strong contrast to the great classic of the fifteenth century, Littleton's *Tenures*, which gives no hint that there were such things as Year Books. (The few apparent exceptions to this statement seem to be interpolations into Littleton's original text.[1])

It is not easy to imagine the attitude of lawyers towards the Year Books. We must be clear that they played little part in the ordinary lawyer's professional work, and in that sense were of little moment; on the other hand, a lawyer who owned some would prize them highly. Thus Richard Banks, a baron of the exchequer, had a 'book of terms' which had once belonged to Sir Robert Plessington, chief baron; Banks seems to have put a high value on it, and by his will dated 1415 he directs it to be kept to the use of his sons and the longest liver of them, and after his death without issue who can profit by the books, to be sold at the best price obtainable and the proceeds given to the poor.[2] We must conclude, I think, that in the fifteenth century the Year Books were esteemed by those lucky enough to possess them, but that the profession as a whole got along quite comfortably without them.

And so the darkness deepened, as far as common-law literature is concerned. It is true that Littleton's *Tenures* is a superlative book and was read with awe and wonder. But one book, however splendid, does not make a literature, and cannot be taken as evidence of the general character of contemporary culture. Beside Littleton there is nothing whatever which can be called a law-book, however feeble, to represent professional writing in his age. The Year Books alone remain, and from that precariously sustained series we learn enough to show that the law was in fact developing steadily and usefully according to its own queer lights. The curious story of 'case' was to give us a law of tort, and from the absurdities of *assumpsit* there was to emerge, painfully and slowly, a law of contract. Judges and serjeants were as keen as ever in wrangling over their incredible points of pleading and procedure, and the legislature was showing faint signs of life, preparatory to its

---

[1] H. S. Bennett, *English Books and Readers*, p. 223 discusses the early printed editions of Littleton, and concludes that lawyers preferred to have corrupt versions of the text.

[2] *The Register of Henry Chichele* (ed. E. F. Jacob), II, 67.

boisterous exploits under Henry VIII. It is an astonishing demonstration that a tightly closed system of customary law, hermetically sealed from all communication with the outer world, may yet continue alive for a considerable period without either using or creating a literature.[1]

Tough the law certainly was, and Maitland divined the secret when he pointed to the teachers as the explanation. Professor Thorne's work has already thrown much new light upon the inns of court, their Readers, their moots, and their readings. It was these picked men whose oral lectures replaced the written book, reminding us of the archaic times when literature was handed on by the spoken word before the use of writing. By the end of the century they get written down, and there are clear signs that the Readers, if no one else, had been looking at the Year Books. They were indeed a slender thread, but it held. It was the Year Books, in this most obscure epoch, which maintained the continuity of English law. There was indeed the sun of Bracton and the moon of Littleton to illuminate the scene each in his season, but for most of the time English lawyers walked by the light of faint anonymous stars. Of science there was very little (and I have been at some pains to lament it rather loudly). Nevertheless, English law plodded on, with its eyes stubbornly turned away from the glittering pages of the Digest to pursue its own course—insular, lay, and French (what French!). Altogether an odd story, which may well arouse our interest; indeed, it fascinated Maitland.

---

[1] The readings at the inns of court were frequently adaptations of earlier ones: *Readings and Moots* (ed. Thorne, Selden Society, vol. LXXI).

INDEX

For EU product safety concerns, contact us at Calle de José Abascal, 56–1°,
28003 Madrid, Spain or eugpsr@cambridge.org.